BUSINESS GOD'S WAY

Howard Dayton

-finances God's way™

www.compass1.org

Dear Tom —

Deeply grateful for your friendship, dear brother!

This book is part of Larry's legacy.

Love in Jesus,

Howard Dayton

To Tim Manor and Jess Correll, your love for Christ and commitment to conduct business His way have inspired and encouraged me for decades. Thankful we are growing old together!

I am deeply grateful for the tireless effort of Bruce Witt, and the prayers and wise counsel of Steve French, Doug Hunter, Tim Krauss, Ben LeVan, Dave Rae, and Carl Tompkins.

To Kyle Hasbrouck, Dan Schilling, Jim Whorton, Yvonne Mitto, Richard Samuel, Andres Panasiuk, Peter Briscoe, Ngee Khoon, and the worldwide Compass family: without your encouragement this never would have been written.

To Dr. Sandra Gray, I so appreciate your vision to create a college that teaches business God's way. And Dean Mike Kane, thank you for making this vision a reality.

Lord Jesus Christ . . . thank You for loving us enough to reveal in the Bible how we should operate a business.

TABLE OF
CONTENTS

GETTING THE MOST FROM THIS BOOK

This book will transform your business.

"Well, Howard," you say, "that's a pretty audacious claim. How can you say that?"

Here's how.

As you begin to learn what the God of the universe has to say about operating a business—and then put those principles to work—God Himself will transform your business, and nobody but nobody does it better than He.

We've all had the experience of reading books, and then a few days later, we can barely remember what we just read.

Don't let *this* book be one of those books.

I urge you to read this book, but more than that, to consume this book. Have you ever seen a book read by someone who really valued the contents? The book is a mess! Its pages are underlined, highlighted, and dog-eared. It has writing in the margins—and maybe even coffee stains on the cover.

That's my prayer for the book you hold in your hands. I pray that you will not only read it, but personalize it. Make it *yours*. The books that have helped me the most are the ones that I interacted with, not just quickly read.

Study this book, or better yet, become part of a small group to encourage one another to apply what you are learning.

Business God's Way includes three features to assist you:

1. Discussion questions. The book is divided into six sections, and at the end of each section are discussion questions. Meet with your friend, group, or leadership team at work to answer the questions, discuss what you read, and bounce ideas off each other. This will help you. No . . . let me restate that. This will help you enormously.

2. Helpful resources. At the end of each section, we have identified for you outstanding organizations, books, tools, videos, and assistance you can access online.

3. The Compass website is created to equip people of all ages to handle money God's way. Log on to the Compass web site and click on the Business tab. It contains excellent business resources, videos, online tools and answers to frequently asked questions. It also has a Genius Bar to connect you with experts in various areas of business.

www.compass1.org

Allow me to add this one personal note: As I wrote this book, I prayed for you. I truly did. No, I may never have the privilege of meeting you personally, but I prayed that each and every person who embarks on this journey would experience the tremendous sense of hope, peace, and encouragement that comes from discovering how to conduct business God's way. I am excited even as I write these words, because I know that great things are in store for you.

So, let's get started together.

Section One: Starting Well

ONE

Where Did He Go to Business School?

Dave Palmer was speechless. He felt like he'd stumbled over a downed power line and received a 12,000-volt jolt.

Scott, the Chairman of the Board, unexpectedly informed Dave that he was no longer employed at the company, effective immediately. Dave was incredulous.

All he could say at first was, "But why? Are you serious?"

Scott angrily told him that three other executives had met with the Board and given them an ultimatum: fire Dave or they would resign.

"But this makes no sense," Dave responded in bewilderment. "Our market share is at an all-time high, we're financially healthy, and we have great new software under development."

Scott, however, refused to discuss it further.

Dave Palmer had been the founder and CEO of this highly successful global software company he had launched from his own garage a quarter century earlier. Dave had been generous to reward the work of others by giving so much of his company's stock to the Board of Directors and leadership team that they now owned a majority of the stock and were in control.

Dave had been grooming three executives looking for his possible successor, and had chosen to be paid less than any of them. Later, Dave learned they had become impatient waiting for him to retire and conspired with the Chairman to fire him.

Devastated, Dave took a year to recover. Then, when the creative juices finally started flowing again, he started a new software company. Although he made a commitment not to initiate recruitment of his former company's employees, many approached him—because the culture of the former company had changed dramatically after his departure. Dave's new business grew steadily.

In less than a decade, his former company's revenues shriveled to less than twenty percent of what they had been when Dave was fired, and it was close to going out of business. Their largest customer became dissatisfied with the performance of their most recent software and asked Dave to become their software provider.

Dave had forgiven Scott and his former leadership team years before and prayed often for them. He felt that God wanted him to help Scott, so he had his software engineers analyze their deficient software. They discovered how it could be improved. Dave called Scott and told him that for no cost he would help improve the software so that he would not lose the customer.

Crazy Christianity! That's what some would say. Others would add, "Insanity! What about greater market share and putting your ruthless competitor out of business? What about the bottom line?"

By now you may be thinking, Where did Dave go to business school and learn to manage his business?

TWO

Business by the Book

Dave Palmer had been grooming his 38 year old son, Adam, to succeed him as CEO of Palmer Software. Dave's decision to help the leadership of their former company bewildered Adam.

"I don't believe this!" Adam had charged into Dave's office, waving a memo in his hand. "How could you do this, Dad? They stole your company! For the last ten years they've lied about us. Slandered us. Tried every way possible to sabotage Palmer Software. And if that's not enough, you're doing this job gratis? Not charging them a penny?"

"I know, I know." Dave leaned back in his chair, and responded quietly. "Look Adam, it won't always make earthly sense trying to operate our business God's way. I get that." He picked up the Bible on his desk. "But we've made a commitment to base our decisions on this book."

It may surprise you to learn how much the Bible—a book written thousands of years ago—has to say about business and finances. More than 2,350 verses address God's way of handling money and possessions, and hundreds of verses have application to operating a business.

The Bible makes these remarkable claims about itself: *"For the word of God is living and active and sharper than any two-edged sword, and . . . able to judge the thoughts and intentions of the heart"* (Hebrews 4:12-13). *"All Scripture is inspired by God and profitable for teaching, for reproof, for correction, for training in righteousness; so that the man of God may be adequate, equipped for every good work"* (2 Timothy 3:16-17). The truths in the Bible are timeless. It is truly a living book that communicates God's direction to all generations, bringing wisdom and perspective to every situation of life.

When we think of people who are skilled in business decision-making, we often think of "experts"—or those who are older and more experienced. Yet the Bible offers us more insight and wisdom than experts or highly-paid consultants who don't know God's way of operating a business. The psalmist wrote, *"Your commands are always with me and make me wiser than my enemies. . . . I have more insight than all my teachers, for I meditate on your statutes"* (Psalm 119:98-99, NIV). *"I understand more than the aged, because I have observed Your precepts"* (Psalm 119:100).

Warning: It's going to be different!

The way most people operate a business stands in sharp contrast to God's business principles. Isaiah 55:8 puts it like this: *"'For my thoughts are not your thoughts, neither are your ways my ways,' declares the Lord"* (NIV). The most significant difference between the two is that the Bible reveals God being closely involved in every area of our lives, including our work. Many people fail to realize this because He has chosen to be invisible to us and to operate in the unseen supernatural realm.

The Bible has more than 2,350 verses that address God's way of handling money and possessions, and hundreds of verses that apply to operating a business.

The next verse says: *"As the heavens are higher than the earth, so are my ways higher than your ways and my thoughts than your thoughts"* (Isaiah 55:9, NIV). Not only are God's ways different, they are exponentially better. (Just how much higher are the heavens than the earth?) So fasten your seatbelt! This book will transform your business, your finances, and your life as you learn what the God of the universe says about operating a business and so much more. This book is for everyone in business—whether the business is large or small, well-established or startup, prosperous or struggling, a for-profit enterprise or a non-profit charity.

WHO OWNS THE BUSINESS?

Soon after starting his first software company, Dave Palmer's perspective of business was radically transformed by participating in a Bible study on money. Not only are we to honor Christ in our company, he thought to himself, but everything we have belongs to God, even the business.

Recognizing this changed everything! He felt as if he had been elevated from the role of just operating *his* business, to the most important position possible—a person entrusted with managing *God's* business. Dave Palmer had embraced the most significant truth for the Christian in business—ownership.

"For my thoughts are not your thoughts, neither are your ways my ways," declares the Lord. "As the heavens are higher than the earth, so are my ways higher than your ways and my thoughts than your thoughts"
Isaiah 55:8-9

God owns it all

The Lord owns everything in the world, including our businesses—public or private, large or small. *"To the Lord your God belong . . . the earth and everything in it"* (Deuteronomy 10:14, NIV). *"The earth is the Lord's, and all it contains"* (Psalm 24:1).

Scripture even reveals specific items God owns.

- Leviticus 25:23 identifies Him as the owner of every square inch of land: *"The land must not be sold permanently, because the land is mine"* (NIV).

- Haggai 2:8 says that He owns precious metals: *"'The silver is Mine, and the gold is Mine,' declares the Lord of hosts."*

- In Psalm 50:10-12, the Scriptures tell us: *"Every beast of the forest is Mine, the cattle on a thousand hills . . . everything that moves in the field is Mine. If I were hungry I would not tell you, for the world is Mine, and all it contains."*

If we are going to be genuine followers of Christ, we must transfer ownership of our businesses to the Lord. *"None of you can be My disciple who does not give up all his own possessions"* (Luke 14:33). When we acknowledge God's ownership, every business decision becomes a spiritual decision.

No longer do we ask, "Lord, what do you want me to do with **my** business?"

Instead, we ask, "Lord, what do You want me to do with **Your** business?"

Wanting to be the owner

When we act as if we are the owner of the business, we often allow it to own us! In 1928, a group of the world's most successful financiers met at the Edgewater Beach Hotel in Chicago. The group read like the Fortune 500: the president of the largest utility company, the greatest wheat speculator, the president of the New York Stock Exchange, a member of the President's Cabinet, the greatest "bear" on Wall Street, the president of the Bank of International Settlements, and the head of the world's greatest monopoly.

Collectively, these tycoons controlled more wealth than there was in the United States Treasury! For years, newspapers and magazines had been printing their success stories and urging the youth of the nation to follow their examples.

Twenty-five years later, this is what happened to these men:

- Charles Schwab, the president of the largest independent steel company, lived on borrowed money the last five years of his life and died broke.

- The greatest wheat speculator, Arthur Cotten, died insolvent.

- The president of the New York Stock Exchange, Richard Whitney, served a term in Sing Sing Prison.

- The member of the President's Cabinet, Albert Fall, was

pardoned from prison so he could die at home.

- The greatest "bear" on Wall Street, Jesse Livermore, committed suicide.

- The president of the Bank of International Settlements, Leon Fraser, committed suicide.

- The head of the world's greatest monopoly, Ivar Drueger, committed suicide.

When these men originally met in 1928, they all thought they alone were responsible for making their fortune. But not one of them understood that Jesus Christ was the owner of their business, and they needed to operate it His way.

We are stewards

Our responsibility is summed up in this verse: *"It is required in stewards that one be found faithful"* (1 Corinthians 4:2, NKJV). A steward is a manager of someone else's possessions. We are managers of the businesses and possessions that the Lord entrusts to us.

Before we can be faithful, we have to step back and gain perspective on what God expects of us. Just as the purchaser of complicated software studies the manufacturer's manual to learn how to operate it, we need to examine the Creator's handbook—the Bible—to determine how He wants us to operate His businesses.

The Framework of this Book

Every successful business has four components that function well: Values, Strategy, People, and Finances. If one is missing or weak, the business will not achieve it's potential. In this book, we will examine how to significantly improve each of these components—all from God's perspective.

See the diagram on the next page for learning *Business God's Way*.

It's been said that the best way to finish well is to start well. This chapter has been all about starting well, which simply means embracing the foundational truths that God owns your business and His way of operating it is the best way.

Business Plan

Few enterprises succeed without a well designed Business Plan. At the end of each Section of this book, you will complete a practical step aimed at improving your existing Business Plan or helping you develop one tailor-made for your business for the very first time. Our goal is for you to gain a sound biblical foundation for your business and a solid business plan. The basic Business Plan you will be completing is also available for free in electronic form at the Compass web site, as well as a more detailed plan.

There are no one-size-fits-all Business Plans. On the contrary, the content and format should be thoughtfully adapted to your business. We encourage you complete this with your leadership team at work.

In this Section, you will complete a SWOT Analysis. Its purpose is to help you evaluate the Strengths, Weaknesses, Opportunities, and Threats to the organization or department. Once these facts have been gathered, it aids in the development of the Business Plan.

With your leadership team, conduct a SWOT Analysis of the business or department.

Strengths:

_____

_____

_____

_____

Weaknesses:

_____

_____

_____

_____

Opportunities:

_____

_____

_____

_____

Threats:

_____

_____

_____

_____

Looking Back at Section 1: Starting Well

React: Let's talk about it

1. Right now, today . . . what are the most challenging issues you face today in your business or career?

2. How do you think the Bible might help you make wise business and financial decisions?

3. Do you consistently recognize that God owns your business? If not, what will you do to be more consistent?

4. What were the most important insights you learned from completing the SWOT Analysis?

5. What will you do to improve any weaknesses in your business or department?

6. What benefits do you hope to receive from reading this book?

Help! – Online and other resources

Business By The Book, by Larry Burkett, Thomas Nelson Publishers, Nashville, TN

Business God's Way small group study, www.compass1.org

Business God's Way DVD Series, www.compass1.org

Section Two: Values

THREE

Vision, Mission, and Values

When Dave Palmer launched Palmer Software, he gathered his leadership team together for the first time and asked them a question.

"Did you ever hear of a successful sports team getting ready for the big game and not developing a game plan?"

He followed that up with another questions.

"Did you ever hear about an army preparing for war and not having a battle plan?"

Obviously, no one had heard of such a thing. Dave went on. "In a similar way, developing a business plan is crucial for the success of our company. A business plan is important—whether you're the owner or CEO of a company or the manager of a department."

Throughout the Bible we are encouraged to plan. *"The plans of the diligent lead to profit as surely as haste leads to poverty"* (Proverbs 21:5, NIV). Let's face it. Planning requires effort, patience, and thought. It's the opposite of making quick, on-the-fly decisions that are often geared to solving immediate problems.

In Luke 14:28-30, Jesus illustrates the importance of planning ahead when He asks, *"For which one of you, when he wants to build a tower, does not first sit down and calculate the cost to see if he has enough to complete it? Otherwise, when he has laid a foundation and is not able to finish, all who observe it begin to ridicule him, saying, 'This man began to build and was not able to finish.'"*

> **"Write your plans in pencil, and then give the Lord the eraser!"**
>
> Author Larry Burkett

Biblical planning begins with recognizing God's role in the business. Proverbs 3:5-6 reads, *"Trust in the Lord with all your heart and do not lean on your own understanding. In all your ways acknowledge Him, and He will make your paths straight."* When drawing up a plan for a startup or an existing business, you should *"in all your ways acknowledge Him"*—that is, welcome Him into every aspect of the enterprise.

We need God's favor and guidance for the business to succeed. Proverbs 16:3 tells us, *"Commit your works to the Lord and your plans will be established."* If we plan apart from seeking the Lord's direction and only ask Him to rubber-stamp our plans, we will soon find ourselves in a dangerous place. We are to plan, but ultimately the Lord controls the outcome. Proverbs 16:9 reveals, *"The mind of man plans his way, but the Lord directs his steps."* Author Larry Burkett observed, "Write your plans in pencil, and then give the Lord the eraser!"

In other words, go ahead and lay out the direction that seems best to you, but always leave the door open for the Lord to make tweaks—or hand you a new plan you'd never even dreamed of.

The Business Plan

Business owners, entrepreneurs, and key managers are often consumed with running the day-to-day operations of their business and overlook developing or implementing a business plan. In the pages of this book, one of our objectives is to help you develop your business plan with enough detail to enable you to achieve your goals. The business plan consists of the four primary components we mentioned before: Values, Strategy, People, and Finances—all built upon the foundation of the truths found in the Bible.

Nehemiah is a terrific example of a person who prepared and executed a business plan well. It all began when he learned that the people of God in Jerusalem were vulnerable to attack by their enemies, because the city's walls were *"broken down and its gates are burned"* (Nehemiah 1:3). Shattered walls and charred gates were a grave security concern in that day.

After carefully evaluating the situation and taking stock of his resources, Nehemiah waded into the chaos and implemented a step-by-step plan to restore order, safety, and hope in that discouraged community.

We can learn a great deal from the steps this wise official took as we begin developing our business plan.

1. Prayer. When Nehemiah learned of the problem, he *"sat down and wept. For some days,* [he] *mourned and fasted and prayed before the God of heaven. . . .* [He said] *'Lord, let your ear be attentive to the prayer of this your servant . . . Give your servant success today by granting him fa-*

vor in the presence of this man.' I was cupbearer to the king" (Nehemiah 1: 4, 11, NIV).

The most critical ingredient in the success of any business is to pray. Period.

This is especially true when starting a business, making crucial decisions, or grappling with a difficulty. Invite the Creator of the universe to give you guidance as you develop the business plan, and expect Him to respond. As we learned in the last chapter, He owns everything, including your business, and wants to be involved as you manage it.

Psalm 127:1 emphasizes the significance of God's role in your business. It says, *"Unless the Lord builds the house, they labor in vain who build it; unless the Lord guards the city, the watchman keeps awake in vain."* Stop reading for a few minutes and ask the Spirit of God to make this truth part of your thinking. Unless the Lord builds and protects your business, unless you allow Him in on the very ground floor of all that you attempt, you're working in vain. That means it will all come up empty! All your work, all your planning, all your sacrifice, all your investment. This is the reason your business must be built on prayer.

When I was in the real estate development business, I realized the importance of confirming that the Lord wanted me to develop a project before launching it, because the financial cost of failure would have been catastrophic. On my last project, that meant literally getting down on my knees on the land of the potential project every day for six months. Finally, the Lord made it clear through a unique set of circumstances that He wanted us to go forward with the development. When you know for certain He is calling you to do something in business, it increases your confidence and courage, and you can experience peace even in the midst of challenges.

2. Purpose. Some months later, the king asked Nehemiah why he was sad. Taking a great risk, Nehemiah responded with candor, saying it was because Jerusalem had been reduced to rubble. *"Then the king said to me, 'What would you request?' So I prayed to the God of heaven. I said to the king . . . 'send me . . . that I may rebuild it.'"* (Nehemiah 2:4-5).

Nehemiah concisely communicated to the king what he wanted to accomplish and why. This was his 30-second elevator speech that summarized his Mission and Vision.

3. Plan. Nehemiah told the king precisely how long he would be gone. Then, he asked the king for letters guaranteeing his safe passage for the long trip and requisitioning the timber needed to rebuild the city gates. It was so obvious that he had thought it all out (and prayed it all out) in advance. Nehemiah had planned ahead and indentified what he would need to be successful.

Vision, Mission, and Values

Every business and organization should have clearly articulated Vision, Mission, and Values. This is the framework from which every decision, large and small, should be made. Companies often define Vision and Mission differently; therefore, you may need to adjust the headings to conform to your definitions.

Vision (or Purpose) Statement

Without a clear vision, people tend to drift away from the real purpose of the business. Proverbs 29:18 says it this way, *"Where there is no vision, the people are unrestrained . . ."* One of the biggest advantages of implementing clear vision, mission, and values is that they will attract the right people to your business—and repel others at the same time. As many of my colleagues and friends could testify down through the years, the only thing worse than being short-handed when you need extra help is hiring the wrong people!

A vision or purpose statement doesn't describe "what we do," it communicates why we exist. It should describe future outcomes, benefits, and what the business will look like. As you review the following vision statements, note carefully the way they define how they want to be viewed by the people and markets they serve. We have included Compass as an example for those who work in a church or non-profit charity.

First Southern National Bank: We will use our example, our influence, and our resources to help others make wise financial decisions.

Alcoa: Our vision is to be the best company in the world—in the eyes of our customers, shareholders, communities and people. We expect and demand the best we have to offer by always keeping Alcoa's values top of mind.

Chick-fil-A: To glorify God by being a faithful steward of all that is entrusted to us and to have a positive influence on all who come in contact with Chick-fil-A.

Compass—*finances God's way*: To see everyone, everywhere, faithfully living by God's financial principles in every area of their lives.

Mission Statement

A business's mission statement describes the primary activity that must occur consistently for a company to be successful. It defines what distinguishes your business and what should influence your effort to fulfill your purpose. When drafting a mission statement for your business or department, make it concise, realistic, and motivating.

The following are examples:

Joe Gibbs Racing: Our goal is to field for our sponsors and fans competitive race cars with the goal of winning races and championships. Our expectation is that we will be able to see in our growth and success, things that would have never been accomplished except by the direct intervention of God.

Walt Disney 's mission statement used to be: To make people happy.

First Southern National Bank: First Southern is a team committed to affirming the dignity and value of all people, being responsible stewards, delivering more than is expected, and making our communities better places in which to live.

Compass—*finances God's way*: Equipping people worldwide to faithfully apply God's financial principles so they may know Christ more intimately, be free to serve Him, and help fund the Great Commission.

Values

A business's values are intended to govern how a business operates and deals with customers, vendors, employees, communities, and other stakeholders. The values help determine priorities and facilitate decision-making.

The following are examples:

First Southern National Bank

Generosity. Giving is huge! We believe in sharing our time, our knowledge and our resources with others.

Relationships. They matter a lot—in our faith, our families, our friendships and our work.

Excellence. We strive for excellence in all we do, and we recognize that it comes only through continuous learning and effort.

Accountability. We believe that we should always do the right thing and we hold ourselves accountable to that.

Teamwork. We succeed as a Team. Personal ambition is important but each of us must be willing to sacrifice it for a Greater Good!

Lockheed Martin

Passion. To be passionate about winning and about our brands, products and people, thereby delivering superior value to our shareholders.

Risk Tolerance. To create a culture where entrepreneurship and prudent risk taking are encouraged and rewarded.

Excellence. To be the best in quality and in everything we do.

Motivation. To celebrate success, recognizing and rewarding the achievements of individuals and teams.

Innovation. To innovate in everything, from products to processes.

Empowerment. To empower our talented people to take the initiative and to do what's right.

Compass—*finances God's way*

Christ Centered. The Lord owns Compass and is the only One who knows the direction we should take. He alone produces transformed lives.

Spirit Led. In the same way that Jesus depended on the Holy Spirit to reveal the will of the Father, we too, are completely dependent on Him to reveal God's will for Compass and for each of us as individuals.

Bible Based. Everything Compass teaches and does must be based on the Word of God.

Prayer Driven. Prayer is essential. Seeking the Lord's direction, provision, and protection through prayer must be a constant focus for us individually and throughout the entire ministry.

Discipleship Focused. Jesus commanded us to "go and make disciples of all nations." This was His priority, and it will be ours.

The Triple Bottom Line

Pete Ochs, the founder of Capital III, is an entrepreneur with manufacturing, real estate, energy, and education companies in the US and Latin America.

Pete named the company Capital III because of his conviction that businesses should have a triple bottom line: economic, social, and spiritual. The *economic* bottom line is created by operating a profitable enterprise. The *social* bottom line occurs when the business uses its financial resources to creatively meet social needs. And the *spiritual* bottom line materializes when the company intentionally uses its platform to influence its employees, vendors, and customers for Christ.

Pete realized that the glue to ensure the businesses would remain focused on accomplishing the triple bottom line were Capital III's Vision, Mission, and Values:

Our Vision is to help change the world through entrepreneurship.

Our Mission is to be an absolutely trusted business.

Our Values are to honor God by serving people, pursuing excellence, and stewarding resources.

In 2009, Capital III bought a bankrupt manufacturing business located in a small rural community. Their biggest dilemma was how to hire enough workers in a town with a very small labor force. To compound the problem, they needed employees that would work a completely flexible schedule—from 20 to 40 hours a week—depending entirely on the volume of business.

Every business managed by followers of Christ should have a triple bottom line: economic, social, and spiritual.

Before anything else— prior to any brainstorming, group discussions, or analysis—Pete and his leadership team prayed and sought the Lord's direction. They made prayer Job One.

Not long after that, an out-of-the-box idea came to them.

They approached the local state-operated correctional facility about utilizing the prison population as the labor force. At the time, inmates were earning only about $7 a day, and Capital III could pay them a starting salary of about $10 an hour. Approximately thirty percent of their wage would be used to reimburse the state for their room and board. The rest they could spend, save, or send to help support their families.

This creative solution has accomplished all three bottom lines.

Economic: Because the labor force is flexible, the company is able to control its labor costs, meet the just-in-time demands of its customers, and reduce inventories, all of which contribute to the profitability of the business. The company also doesn't need to compensate the work force with paid vacation time! Inmates can earn up to $100 per day, 14 times as much as they did while working for the state.

Social: The state and taxpayers benefit because a portion of what the prisoners earn defrays the cost of room and board. Prisoners are motivated to behave well while in prison, because anyone involved with a disciplinary problem is not eligible to work for Capital III. The prisoners also learn marketable skills that will help them earn a living once they are released from prison. Interestingly, the inmates have chosen to send a majority of what they receive in salary to help support their families.

Spiritual: Capital III is committed to treating the work force with respect and to help them in practical ways. They are helping to build a spiritual life center at the prison, in which life skill classes and Bible studies are conducted. Capital III also has been instrumental in starting a seminary inside the prison. The business also provides periodic meals and get-togethers for the workers and their families. Every two weeks, Capital III provides motivational and inspirational programs for its workers. In short, the workers have been valued and loved. This has influenced many to consider Christ as their Savior.

Pete Ochs has a big vision. He is praying for the Lord to replicate this model of valuing people and creating economic, social, and spiritual capital in businesses across America and around the world.

FOUR

Seeking Counsel

T he Lord encourages us to seek counsel.

Proverbs 12:15 says, *"The way of a fool is right in his own eyes, but a wise man is he who listens to counsel."* Receiving timely counsel is fundamental to operating a successful business. The collective IQ of a team is especially helpful when developing and implementing a business plan.

Before making an important business decision, subject it to three sources of counsel.

1. The counsel of the Lord

In Isaiah 9:6, we are told that one of the Lord's names is *"Wonderful Counselor."* The Psalms identify God as our counselor. *"I* [the Lord] *will instruct you and teach you in the way which you should go; I will counsel you with my eye upon you"* (Psalm 32:8). *"You* [Lord] *guide me with your counsel"* (Psalm 73:24, NIV).

The Lord's counsel comes to us through prayer, directly from His Word, and indirectly through others. It is important to remember that only the Lord can reveal truth and proper direction. Only the Lord knows the future and the ultimate consequences of a business decision.

In Zephaniah 1:6, the Lord reveals that He will judge *"those who have turned their back from following the LORD, and those who have not sought the LORD or inquired of Him."* God wants us to ask Him for guidance and to follow Him.

It always helps to step back and consider the big picture. And here it is: The Lord intends for us to use our work to help us grow closer to Jesus Christ. Throughout Scripture we are encouraged to wait upon our heavenly Father. He invites us to simply sit quietly and express to Him our gratitude and love. He wants us to share our needs and concerns and ask for His direction. So, whenever you feel hurried or pressured or you experience a sense of confusion concerning a business decision, go to a quiet place that will allow you to pray and listen for His still, small voice.

The big picture: The Lord intends for us to use our work to help us grow closer to Jesus Christ.

---

2. Counsel of the Bible

As we discovered in the first chapter, the Bible is a living book that the Lord uses to communicate His wisdom and direction to all generations.

It is never irrelevant.

It is never dated.

The psalmist wrote, *"Your laws are both my light and my counselors"* (Psalm 119:24, TLB). Taking this truth to heart, learn what God's Word says about a particular issue. Look for timeless biblical principles that apply to your situation. If Scripture clearly answers a question, you don't have to go any further because the Bible contains the Lord's written, revealed will.

Unfortunately, the majority of business people who know Christ are not daily Bible readers. Romans 10:17 says, *"So faith comes from hearing, and hearing by the word of Christ."* If you want to know Christ well and learn His ways, there is no substitute for spending consistent, thoughtful time in God's word, the Bible.

Even when the Bible clearly speaks to an issue, however, and gives us clear direction, we still have the option to compromise that truth or reject it out of hand. I have learned the hard way that this is just plain dumb!

If, however, the Bible doesn't speak specifically to a given issue, we should seek the third source of counsel: godly people.

3. Counsel of godly people

Proverbs 15:22 reads, *"Without consultation, plans are frustrated, but with many counselors they succeed."* And Proverbs 11:14 adds, *"Where there is no guidance the people fall, but in abundance of counselors there is victory."*

Each of us has a limited range of knowledge and experience. Whether we know it or not and whether we admit it or not, we need the input of others. We need their unique backgrounds to give us insight and stimulate our thinking with alternatives we would never have considered without their advice.

Are you surrounding yourself with wise counsel? In a business, these counselors may be your Board of Directors, your leadership team, or even outside consultants.

It's also helpful to meet regularly with a small group of peers who aren't associated directly with your business to share your lives, pray for one another, and be accountable to each other. You will experience the benefits and safety of having a group of people who know you, love you, and give you objective counsel . . . even when it hurts. I am more receptive to constructive criticism when it comes from someone who I know cares for me.

Seeking your spouse's counsel

"Adam, the biggest mistake I've ever made in business," confided Dave Palmer, "was not listening to my wife when she told me she was uneasy when around some of those in leadership at our former company. She didn't have any concrete evidence that they would eventually betray me, but intuitively she didn't trust them. I didn't pay enough attention to her. I wish with all my heart that I had!"

If you are married, the first person to consult is your spouse. Frankly, in the beginning of our marriage, it was hard for me to seek Bev's counsel in financial and business matters. After all, she had no formal business training. But I began to see that her wise advice saved us a boatload of money.

Women tend to be gifted with a wonderfully sensitive nature that is usually very accurate. Men tend to focus on the facts. Couples need each other to achieve the proper balance for an optimal decision. I believe the Lord honors the wife's role as helper to her husband. Many times the Lord communicates most clearly to a husband through his wife.

Husbands, listen to me. Regardless of her financial aptitude, you need to listen to your wife's counsel—*particularly in people matters.* I committed never to proceed with any sizable business decision without my wife's agreement, and it has saved our financial bacon more than once! I recall preparing to make a large business investment that Bev didn't feel comfortable with. Because of her reluctance, I pulled the plug on the deal. It later went sour, and we would have lost more than $500,000 had I not heeded her advice.

It's important for husbands and wives to agree on big decisions because they will both experience the consequences. Even if the choice a couple makes together proves to be disastrous, their agreement up-front protects their relationship by leaving no grounds for an "I told you so" response. When a couple seeks each other's advice, they are actually communicating, "I love you. I respect you. I value your insight."

The Bible is also clear, however, that we need to carefully *avoid* one particular source of counsel. *"How blessed is the man who does not walk in the counsel of the wicked . . ."* (Psalm 1:1). The word "blessed" literally means to be "happy many times over." The definition of a "wicked" person is one who lives life without regard to God.

In our opinion, it is permissible to seek input from those who may not know Christ for facts and technical expertise, but you are responsible to make the final decision.

Startups and Entrepreneurs

I was completely confused and discouraged. I sensed the Lord wanted me to start a real estate development company, but that meant transitioning from a business I knew well to one I had no experience in and knew very little about. This was going to be far too risky a venture.

Then, the Lord graciously brought me a mentor. He was a godly man with decades of successful real estate development experience. I learned more about the business in two years than I would have in ten trying to do it on my own. He was a walking Wikipedia of how to do things with excellence and avoid costly mistakes. After two years of picking his brain, I felt as if I'd earned a PhD in real estate development.

If you are contemplating a business startup—or you find yourself in the midst of one—it's imperative that you pray for the Lord to send you a mentor. This can mean the difference between success and failure. In fact, I believe all of us would benefit by having a seasoned mentor, someone who has experienced challenging times as well as success. So, ask the Lord to provide you with just the right person, one who has operated their business God's way.

As you mature in your faith in Christ and become experienced in operating a business God's way, you too can serve as a mentor. There are few activities more gratifying than helping an eager learner.

Business Plan

As we have learned, there are many benefits from creating a well-conceived Business Plan. It provides a clear sense of direction for the organization and reduces uncertainties. It helps allocate funds and personnel in the most effective way. It minimizes impulsive decisions by enabling managers to think strategically, while improving the business's ability to adapt to change and grasp appropriate opportunities.

In this Section, you will complete your Vision, Mission, and Values portion of your Business Plan.

Vision, Mission, and Values

What is your Vision Statement?

_____

_____

_____

What is your Mission Statement?

_____

_____

_____

List your Business Values.

1. _____

_____

_____

2. _____

_____

_____

3. _____

_____

_____

4. _____

_____

_____

5. _____

_____

_____

6. _____

_____

_____

Looking Back at Section 2: Values

React: Let's talk about it

1. What did you learn from working on your business's vision, mission, and values?

2. What do you hope to accomplish by implementing the vision, mission, and values?

3. How do you think creating a Business Plan or refining one will benefit your company?

4. Do you consistently seek counsel from other people? If not, what prevents you?

5. What do you think about the concept of implementing the three bottom lines (economic, social, and spiritual) in your business?

6. Describe how you believe the three bottom lines would be best accomplished in your business.

Help! – Online and other resources

Good to Great, by Jim Collins, Harper Collins Publishers

Section Three: Strategy

FIVE

My Business is My Pulpit

Despite what many believe, God hard wired us to work.

Work was initiated for our benefit in the sinless environment of the garden of Eden, it's not a result of the curse! *"The Lord God took the man and put him into the garden of Eden to cultivate it and keep it"* (Genesis 2:15).

The very first thing the Lord did with Adam was to put him to work.

After the fall, work became more difficult. *"Cursed is the ground because of you; in toil you will eat of it all the days of your life. Both thorns and thistles it shall grow for you; and you will eat the plants of the field; by the sweat of your face you will eat bread . . ."* (Genesis 3:17-19).

Work is so important that God gives us this command in Exodus 34:21: *"You shall work six days . . ."* The apostle Paul is just as direct: *"If anyone is not willing to work, then he is not to eat"* (2 Thessalonians 3:10). Examine the verse carefully. It says, *"If anyone is not **willing** to work."* It does not say, *"If anyone **cannot** work."* This principle does not apply to those who are physically or mentally unable to work; it is for those who are able but choose not to work.

The Lord intends our work and involvement in business to develop our character. While the CEO of a construction company is building a housing subdivision, the subdivision is also building the CEO. The CEO's skills, diligence, integrity, and judgment are refined. A business and job aren't merely designed to earn money; they are also intended to produce godly character in the life of the worker.

Business is Honorable

According to the Bible, there is equal dignity in all types of honest businesses and work. The Scripture does not elevate any profession above another; we find in its pages a wide variety of vocations. David was a shepherd and a king. Lydia was a retailer who sold purple fabric. Daniel was a government worker. Amos was a shepherd, and tended sycamore fig trees. Mary was a homemaker. Paul operated a tent-making business. And the Lord Jesus Himself was a carpenter.

In fact, most of the godly people in the Bible had secular jobs. In Hebrews 11, there is a list of sixteen men and women who lived by faith and gained God's approval. Only one, Samuel, was a religious professional.

Many feel they are not serving Christ in a significant way if they remain in business. Nothing could be further from the truth! In his book *God Owns My Business*, Stanley Tam writes, "Although I believe in the application of good principles in business, I place far more confidence in the conviction that I have a call from God. I am convinced that His purpose for me is in the business world. **My business is my pulpit**."

God strategically places His children everywhere. Many believe that only the missionary or pastor is truly spiritual, but this isn't true. **Your business is your ministry.** The businessperson is in a position to influence people for Christ who would rarely consider attending a church.

Robert Gilmour "R.G." LeTourneau was 14 years old when he dropped out of the sixth grade. A decade later, he and his wife were broke and heavily in debt from a failed automobile dealership.

His sister, a missionary, challenged him to make a real difference for Christ. LeTourneau was confused and felt guilty because he thought that he would have to become a missionary and give up what he wanted to do—move dirt. Finally, he yielded his will to the Lord and prayed, "Lord, if You'll help me, I'll do anything You want me to do." LeTourneau knew his prayer was answered, because he was overcome with joy.

> *"Although I believe in the application of good principles in business, I place far more confidence in the conviction that I have a call from God. I am convinced that His purpose for me is in the business world. My business is my pulpit." – Stanley Tam*

The next day, he met with his pastor to seek direction. After praying together for some time, the pastor finally said, "R.G., the Lord needs preachers and missionaries, but God needs businessmen, too."

LeTourneau was stunned. If God needed businessmen, he could easily find a better one than a dirt mover buried under a mountain of debt. Finally he reasoned, *Well, if that's what God wants me to be, I'll be His businessman.* From that day on, he was in business with God.

LeTourneau began to tinker with earth-moving machinery, and proved to be extraordinarily innovative. He started manufacturing heavy construction machinery, and the company became enormously successful. In 1935, at the suggestion of his wife, they decided to give 90 percent of the company's profits to the Lord. LeTourneau explained this decision: "It's not how much of *my* money I give to God, but how much of *God's* money I keep for myself."

During World War II, his company built 70 percent of all earth-moving equipment used by the Allies. He registered more than 300 patents, and there isn't a piece of heavy construction equipment manufactured today that did not find its origin on R.G. LeTourneau's drafting table.

The Big Question

When I was in the real estate business, I felt as if I was just as much in full-time ministry as a pastor. When I sold my business and started what became Compass, the only thing that felt different was that I had more time to devote to ministry.

So, there is one question you must answer.

Don't rush to answer it. Take your time.

If God wants me to serve Him in business, am I willing to be His businessperson? If your answer is YES, the rest of this book will provide you the framework that you'll need to operate your business God's way.

SIX

God's Part and Our Part

You've already learned that God owns your business, and that He has entrusted you to be a faithful steward of it. Scripture reveals three additional responsibilities the Lord has in business. Don't skim over these quickly. Spend enough time to embrace the different facets of God's role in whatever your enterprise might be.

God Gives Job Skills.

Exodus 35:30-35 illustrates this truth: *"The LORD has called by name Bezalel . . . and He has filled him with the Spirit of God, in wisdom, in understanding and in knowledge and in all craftsmanship; to make designs for working in gold and in silver and in bronze . . . to perform in every inventive work. He also has put in his heart to teach, both he and*

Oholiab . . . He has filled them with skill to perform every work of an engraver and of a designer and of an embroiderer . . ."

God has given each of us unique aptitudes. People have a wide variety of abilities, manual skills, and intellectual capacities. It's not a matter of one person being better than another. Not at all! It's rather that each has received different abilities. The Lord gives you the abilities to fulfill your God-given role in business, whether you are an entrepreneur, salesperson, or manager.

God Gives Success.

The life of Joseph is an example of God helping a person succeed. *"The LORD was with Joseph, so he became a successful man. . . . His master saw that the LORD was with him and how the LORD caused all that he did to prosper"* (Genesis 39:2-3). The Lord's role in Nehemiah's restoration of the walls of Jerusalem was so evident that he reported, *"So the wall was completed . . . in fifty-two days. When all our enemies heard of it, and all the nations surrounding us saw it, they lost their confidence; for they recognized that this work had been accomplished with the help of our God"* (Nehemiah 6:15-16). Although we all have certain responsibilities, it is ultimately God who controls success.

God Controls Promotions.

Psalm 75:6-7 says, *"For promotion and power come from nowhere on earth, but only from God"* (TLB). Does that surprise you? Our bosses aren't the ones who control whether we'll be promoted. Many people leave God out of work, believing they alone are responsible for their abilities and success. One of the major reasons they experience stress and frustration in their jobs is because they don't understand God's role in work.

Interestingly, promotions often occur after a person remains faithful during deeply challenging circumstances. Joseph was sold into slavery by his jealous brothers and was a prisoner for years before being promoted to Prime Minister of

God gives you the abilities to fulfill your God-given role in business, whether you are an entrepreneur, salesperson, or manager.

Egypt. Daniel faced death in the lion's den before being promoted to the king's right hand. Consider this question for a few minutes: If God gives you your abilities and controls success and promotion, how should this perspective affect your work?

Our Part in Business

Did you know that in business we actually serve the Lord? If you could find a firm grip on this one concept, it would literally change every day of your working life. Paul writes: *"Whatever you do, do your work heartily, as for the Lord rather than for men . . . It is the Lord Christ whom you serve"* (Colossians 3:23-24).

Recognizing that we work for the Lord has profound implications. If you could see Jesus Christ as your boss, would you operate any part of your business differently? The most important question you need to answer every day as you begin your work is this: "For whom do I work?" The Bible makes it clear; the person who signs your paycheck is *not* your ultimate employer.

"Whatever you do, do your work heartily, as for the Lord rather than for men . . . It is the Lord Christ whom you serve" (Colossians 3:23-24).

No matter where you are, you work for Christ Himself.

No matter what you do, be it the president of a company, selling real estate, or managing an assembly line, you work for the Son of God, your Creator and the Lord of the universe.

Work Hard.

Scripture encourages hard work and diligence. *"Whatever your hand finds to do, do it with all your might . . ."* (Ecclesiastes 9:10, NIV). *"The precious possession of a man is diligence"* (Proverbs 12:27). Laziness, however, is strongly condemned: *"He who is slack in his work is brother to him who destroys"* (Proverbs 18:9).

Paul's life was an example of hard work. *"With labor and hardship we kept working night and day so that we might not be a burden to any of you . . . in order to offer ourselves as a model for you, so that you would follow our example"* (2 Thessalonians 3:8-9).

Your work should never be at such a level that people will equate laziness with God. Nothing less than hard work and the pursuit of doing the job well pleases Him. He doesn't require us to be "super-workers" who labor around the clock and never make mistakes, but He does expect us to pursue our responsibilities —whatever they may be— with diligence and integrity.

Leaders should try to motivate lazy employees. During World War II, after a number of pilots died when their chutes didn't open, General George S. Patton discovered he had a problem with lazy parachute packers. An inspection found that one in four chutes was improperly packed.

Enraged, General Patton jumped into action. He paid a surprise visit to the parachute-packing depot and commanded the packers to strap on the last chute they had packed. He immediately drove them to a waiting airplane and had them jump from 7,000 feet. He never again had a packing problem.

But Don't Overwork!

Hard work, however, must be balanced by the other priorities in life. If your business demands so much of your time and energy that you neglect your relationship with Christ or your loved ones, then you're working too much. If you find that your relationship with Christ, your spouse, or your children is suffering, sit down with your spouse and ask yourself a direct question or two. Is the job itself too demanding, or do certain work habits need adjustment?

Management expert Peter Drucker taught that executives need blocks of uninterrupted time to make wise decisions. Truly effective executives realize they need rest and time to pray, think, and plan.

Exodus 34:21 reads, *"You shall work six days, but on the seventh day you shall rest; even during plowing time and harvest you shall rest."* We believe this Old Testament principle of resting one day out of seven is designed for our benefit today. This has been difficult for me, particularly during times of "plowing" or "harvest," when a project deadline approaches or I'm under financial pressure.

Management expert Peter Drucker taught that executives need blocks of uninterrupted time to make wise decisions. Truly effective executives realize they need rest and time to pray, think, and plan. Just think of the incredible changes during the last couple of decades that have made this more difficult.

We've gone from snail mail to email to text messaging. People understood that a response to a letter was going to require days. The average response time for an e-mail, however, is 90 minutes—and 90 seconds for a text message! Who can deny that life is speeding up? It's as though we're on a treadmill where the belt keeps running faster and faster by the minute. Nine out of ten Americans always keep their cell phones within reach. We are constantly barraged with interruptions.

When you think about it, rest can really become an issue of *faith.*

Is the Lord able to make our six days of work more productive than seven? Of course He is! Our Creator instituted weekly rest for our physical, mental, and spiritual health. It's a day a week that we can focus much of our time on getting to know the Lord even better. Philippians 3:8, 10 emphasize the importance of this: *"I consider everything a loss because of the surpassing worth of knowing Christ Jesus my Lord . . . I want to know Christ—yes, to know the power of his resurrection . . . becoming like him in his death"* (NIV).

SEVEN

What's Our Purpose

Here is the big picture of what the Lord wants to accomplish in your business life:

God intends for you to use your business experience to honor and glorify Him and grow closer to Jesus Christ.

God has designed business as a journey—with all its challenges, disappointments, and successes—in which we are to glorify Him. First Corinthians 10:31 says, *"Whether you eat or drink or whatever you do, do all to the glory of God."* And that includes our business lives.

Jesus glorified God. *"I have brought you* [God the Father] *glory on earth by finishing the work you gave me to do"* (John 17:4, NIV). And how did Jesus finish His work? He tells us in John 6:38, *"For I have come down from heaven, not to do My own will, but the will of Him who sent Me."* He did it by obeying His heavenly Father.

How do we accomplish this in our world?

The only way we can glorify the Lord in business is to conduct it without compromise, according to the truths revealed in God's Word. That is why this book is so important. After completing it, you will know what the Bible says about business. However, it's not just *knowing* these things that glorify God; it's *doing* them. James 1:23-25 describes it this way, *"Anyone who listens to the word but does not do what it says is like someone who looks at his face in a mirror and . . . goes away and immediately forgets what he looks like. But whoever looks intently into the perfect law that gives freedom, and continues in it—not forgetting what they have heard,* **but doing it**—*they will be blessed in what they do"* (NIV, emphasis added).

Three Bottom Lines

As we learned earlier, there are three bottom lines in business: economic, social, and spiritual.

Economic Bottom Line

Isaiah 48:17 tells us, *"Thus says the LORD, your redeemer, the holy One of Israel, 'I am the Lord your God, who teaches you to profit, who leads you in the way you should go.'"*

A business should make a profit. If it can't produce a profit, it won't be able to grow, hire employees, or pay vendors. Ultimately, it will fail.

Every follower of Christ in business should work to generate profits, but never by compromising God's way of operating a business. For example, never improve the financial bottom line by marketing dishonestly or taking unfair advantage of employees.

God has designed business as a journey—with all its challenges, disappointments, and successes—in which we are to glorify Him.

There are many reasons why businesses are unprofitable—fierce competition, lack of skilled employees, onerous government regulations, insufficient capital, ineffective administration, changes in the business climate—the list goes on and on.

Other businesses never reach their potential because they are saddled with too much debt, or they try to grow faster than they can develop competent leadership. Some companies suffer because an owner's compensation and lifestyle are more than the business can afford.

A commitment to operating a profitable business begins by carefully building a solid financial foundation. *"Steady plodding brings prosperity"* (Proverbs 21:5, TLB).

Social Bottom Line

The *social* bottom line occurs when the business uses its financial resources and influence to meet social needs. Assess the needs of your community or even the world. Is there a creative way your company can help solve problems and even be a blessing to others?

First Southern Bancorp's home office is located in Stanford, Kentucky, a small rural community. As in many cities, the downtown area was declining rapidly because it was losing business to large retailers on the outskirts of town. The leadership of the bank became committed to revitalizing Stanford.

They started by buying a vacant building next to their bank and completely restoring it. They became the catalyst for a stunning transformation of their town that took place over the next three decades. New retail businesses, a world-class restaurant, and a growing number of renovated buildings anchor the quaint downtown. Tourists are discovering Stanford, and the area is thriving.

Ask the Lord to reveal to you how your business can develop a healthy social bottom line.

Spiritual Bottom Line

The *spiritual* bottom line takes place when a portion of the business's profits are given to help fund the work of God, and people use their business platform to influence others for Christ.

Generosity should characterize Christians in business. Often, the Lord has entrusted them with the spiritual gift of giving. When business men and women understand that they are strategic in funding the work of Christ, their work takes on eternal significance.

The Lord has also given you an opportunity to influence your employees, vendors, customers, and competitors by living for Christ in your company. Someone recently described businesspeople as the "new clergy" because fewer and fewer people are attending church.

Business men and women have a better opportunity to reach people for Christ in the marketplace rubbing shoulders with them five days a week than many pastors influencing them just one morning a week.

Startups and Entrepreneurs

What was the difference between Ray Krock and the McDonald brothers, Richard and Maurice? Krock was a milkshake machine salesman, and the McDonald brothers owned one fast food hamburger restaurant.

The McDonald brothers used to measure the daily sales in the hundreds of hamburgers they sold. In 1995, Ray Krock bought the McDonald brothers' restaurant and started franchising it. McDonalds now measures the number of hamburgers it has sold in the billions.

The difference was leadership, vision, and strategy.

Godly leaders should be learners. We learn four ways:

- *From experience*
- *From other entrepreneurs*
- *From reading books, listening to audio books, viewing DVDs, and participating in seminars or conferences.*
- *From the Lord Himself as you pray and invest time in reading God's word*

If you are not already a learner, I want to encourage you as strongly as possible to become a life-long learner. Leadership author John Maxwell said it this way, "We cannot become what we need to be by remaining what we are."

Business Plan

Business Status and Strategy

Now, you will identify your Business Status and Strategy. It will be very helpful if your leadership team at work can participate in this effort.

As we discovered earlier, Nehemiah's Goal was clear: Rebuild the destroyed wall and gates to protect the citizens of Jerusalem. His Product and/or Service Plan was also clear: Transform burned rubble into a protective wall and repair the gates. The Operations Plan was to motivate and engage the inhabitants of Jerusalem in the rebuilding of the wall.

"Thus says the LORD, your redeemer, the holy One of Israel, 'I am the LORD your God, who teaches you to profit, who leads you in the way you should go'" (Isaiah 48:17).

By today's standards, Nehemiah's use of technology was primitive—but effective. In his day, it was literally cutting edge. There was no heavy machinery, but the builders used trowels and *"each wore his sword girded at his side as he built . . ."* (Nehemiah 4:18). While there were no smart phones to communicate, the trumpeter stood near Nehemiah with the instructions, *"At whatever place you hear the sound of the trumpet, rally to us there. Our God will fight for us"* (Nehemiah 4:20).

Business Status

If a new business startup, summarize why the business is viable.

_____

_____

_____

If an existing business, describe the current status of the business.

_____

_____

_____

Business Defined

What is the business? Describe what the business does or will do.

_____

_____

_____

Identify your primary product or service, its uniqueness, and its benefit to the customer.

_____

_____

_____

How is the business ownership structured (or how will it be)?

_____

_____

_____

Who is your customer?

_____

_____

_____

What is your business model (how it creates, delivers, and makes a profit)?

_____

_____

_____

Describe your Value Proposition (a promise to customers that they will receive value).

_____

_____

_____

Business Goals

What are your short-term goals for the business?

_____

_____

_____

What are your mid-term goals for the business?

_____

_____

_____

What are your long-term goals for the business?

_____

_____

_____

Product and/or Service Plan

Describe your current product and/or service goals:

_____

_____

_____

Describe your mid-term product and/or service goals:

_____

_____

_____

Describe your long-term produce and/or service goals:

_____

_____

_____

What is your strategy to accomplish these goals?

_____

_____

_____

Other plans for your product and/or service:

_____

_____

_____

Operations Plan

Describe your operations and your current infrastructure and systems.

_____

_____

_____

Describe your current operations goals and your plans to accomplish them.

_____

_____

_____

Describe your mid-term operation goals and your plans to accomplish them.

_____

_____

_____

Describe your long-term operations goals and your plans to accomplish them.

_____

_____

_____

Other plans for operations:

_____

_____

_____

Technology Plan

Describe your current use of technology.

_____

_____

_____

How do you plan to use technology effectively mid-term?

_____

_____

_____

How do you plan to use technology effectively long-term?

_____

_____

_____

Looking Back at Section 3: Strategy

React: Let's talk about it

1. What did you learn about the three bottom lines (economic, social, and spiritual) that was particularly helpful of challenging? Describe how you will apply what you learned.

2. Describe how you think you can best glorify the Lord in your business?

3. For whom do you really work? How will this understanding change your attitude toward work and your performance?

4. Are you a hard worker? (Rate yourself on a scale of 1-10, with 10 being the hardest worker. If you work ethic needs improvement, what do you plan to do?

5. Do you get enough rest, and how do you guard against overwork? If you are married, how would your spouse answer this question?

6. What did you learn from completing your business strategy portion of your business plan? What will you do to implement what you discovered?

Help! – Online and other resources

EntreLeadership, by Dave Ramsey, Simon & Schuster Publishers

Section Four: People

EIGHT

Only One Leader

We have already learned some radical things about the Lord's involvement in our business.

— God owns it.

— God controls the circumstances that impact it.

— God counsels us on its direction.

— God determines its ultimate success.

— God gives us the skills and abilities to accomplish our tasks.

Now, we will examine a truth possibly even more amazing.

In fact, it's called a mystery.

"The mystery that has been kept hidden for ages and generations, but is now disclosed to the Lord's people . . . which is Christ in you, the hope of glory" (Colossians 1:26-27, NIV). If you know Jesus Christ as your Savior, He lives **in** you!

The Lord is looking for leaders who are different: Leaders who don't rely upon their charisma, education, hard work, and skills. Business leaders who don't just trust on their strength and willpower to make things happen. He is searching for leaders who are different inside and out, who stand apart from those who have a lukewarm commitment to God.

Most business leaders are not motivated by the desire to serve Christ and care for people. Instead, they use others to achieve their own agenda. They enjoy the power, prestige, and prosperity so often associated with business leadership.

But it's different for those of us who love and serve Jesus Christ.

He is what motivates us.

He is the One who enables us to lead.

Matthew 23:10 says, *"Do not be called leaders; for One is your Leader, that is, Christ."* Stop for a moment, and let that sink in. **There is only one leader, and it isn't you!** Christ invites you to submit to Him as Lord and allow Him to lead through your life.

Just as all spiritual life flows from Christ, so all godly business leadership flows from Him as well. In John 15:5 Jesus said, *"I am the vine, you are the branches; he who abides in Me and I in him, he bears much fruit, for apart from Me you can do nothing."*

So how much can you really accomplish apart from Christ?

Nothing. Zero. Nada. Zilch.

True God-honoring leadership does not spring from our own limited human resources, but from His unlimited supernatural resources.

Many leaders who know Christ want to do things *for* Him, as if He needs our help, our paycheck, or our expertise.

Here's a newsflash: He doesn't. He never has.

The leadership that interests God is His leadership *through* us, rather than our work and leadership *for* Him. This type of leadership flows out of a person's vibrant, intimate relationship with the living God.

Carefully read Galatians 2:20. *"I have been crucified with Christ; and it is no longer I who live, but Christ lives in me; and the life which I now*

Matthew 23:10 says, ***"Do not be called leaders; for One is your Leader, that is, Christ." Stop for a moment, and let that sink in. There is only one leader, and it isn't you!***

live in the flesh I live by faith in the Son of God who loved me and gave Himself up for me." Let's examine this verse through the lens of a businessperson.

- *"I have been crucified with Christ; and it no longer I who live . . ."* I am to be dead to my desires and surrender the leadership of the business and my work to Christ.

- *"but Christ lives in me . . . "* God Himself lives in all those who know Christ.

- *"and the life which I now live in the flesh I live by faith in the Son of God . . ."* I am to yield my life and leadership abilities to Christ and invite him to lead through me.

- *"who loved me and gave Himself up for me."* I can submit to God with confidence because Christ loves me—and demonstrated His love by dying on the cross for me.

Unconditional Surrender

On September 4, 1945, World War II in the Pacific officially ended when Japan unconditionally surrendered to General Douglas MacArthur and the Allies on the U.S.S. Missouri. In war, unconditional surrender involves the defeated submitting fully to the will of the victorious. The vanquished have no choice.

We who know Christ are called to surrender our will unconditionally to the Lord. God, however, has given us the freedom to choose whether to surrender. Unlike those conquered in war, our decision to surrender is motivated by the Lord's unconditional love for us. Our surrender is an act of worship. *"I urge you, brothers and sisters, in view of God's mercy, to offer your bodies as a living sacrifice, holy and pleasing to God—this is your true and proper worship"* (Romans 12:1, NIV).

Christian leaders have long recognized the importance of this total surrender. Dwight L. Moody, founder of Moody Bible Institute, once said, "The world has yet to see what can happen through a person fully committed to doing God's will." Dawson Trotman, founder of the Navigators, added, "God can do more through one person who is 100 percent committed to Him than through 99 who are only partially committed."

> *The leadership that interests God is His leadership through us, rather than our work and leadership for Him. This type of leadership flows out of a person's vibrant relationship with the living God.*

The primary requirement of a godly business leader is unconditional surrender to follow and obey the Lord as an empty, clean vessel for His use. Someone once said, "The main thing is to keep the main thing the main thing." And the main thing for the leader who knows Christ is to surrender and follow Him.

Jesus Christ Modeled Surrender.

In the life of Christ, we see that He completely humbled and submitted Himself to His Heavenly Father, so that God was free to work powerfully through Him. Here are some examples of Christ humbling Himself to His

Father. Note how often Jesus used the words *nothing* and *not* referring to Himself.

- *"The Son can do **nothing** of Himself"* (John 5:19).

- *"I* [Jesus] *can do **nothing** on My own initiative. As I hear, I judge; and My judgment is just, because I do **not** seek My own will, but the will of Him who sent Me"* (John 5:30).

- *"I* [Jesus] *have come down from heaven, **not** to do My own will, but the will of Him who sent Me"* (John 6:38).

- *"My* [Jesus] *teaching is **not** Mine, but His who sent Me"* (John 7:16).

Are You Willing To Surrender?

Jesus was willing to surrender to God, and He tells us in Luke 9:23, *"If anyone wishes to come after Me, he must deny himself, and take up his cross daily and follow Me."*

It requires nothing less than a transformation of our hearts to submit to Christ as Lord and Leader of our business life. Because defense of our own pride and the world's perspective of leadership are so deeply ingrained in most of us, it can require

"God can do more through one person who is 100 percent committed to Him than through 99 who are only partially committed." – Dawson Trotman, founder of the Navigators

years and often difficult circumstances to completely humble ourselves and embrace God's way of leadership.

God knows everything about you, and He is constantly thinking about you. *"You have searched me, LORD, and you know me. You know when I sit and when I rise . . . you are familiar with all my ways. Before a word is on my tongue you, LORD, know it completely . . . Your eyes saw my un-formed body; all the days ordained for me were written in your book be-fore one of them came to be. How precious to me are your thoughts, God! How vast is the sum of them! Were I to count them, they would outnumber the grains of sand"* (Psalm 139:1-4, 16-18, NIV).

The Lord not only knows you perfectly, but because of His great love for you, He wants the best for you. Jeremiah 29:11-13 tells us, *"'For I know the plans I have for you,' declares the Lord, 'plans to prosper you and not harm you, plans to give you hope and a future'"* (NIV). Our Heavenly Father knows what we need to become His leader. He understands that sometimes our character is best developed in adversity. The circumstances may be difficult, painful and lonely. I know! Bev and I have been walked those desolate stretches of road in our lives together. But those trying, sometimes-heartbreaking life situations are intended to draw us into a deeper relationship with Christ.

We have a choice. We can respond by either accepting and learning or fighting and fleeing. As we learn to submit to Christ alone, we experience a reality beyond anything we've known before.

Jesus actually begins to live His life through us.

Servant Leadership

Only once did Jesus say He was leaving His disciples an example—when *"he poured water into a basin and began to wash his disciples' feet"* (John 13:5, NIV). Jesus modeled what He expects of all those in a leadership role—servant leadership. He contrasted the difference between the world's customary practices and God's revolutionary concept of leadership in Mark 10:42-43. *"Those who are recognized as rulers of the Gentiles lord it over them; and their great men exercise authority over them. But it is not* [to be] *this way among you, but whoever wishes to become great among you shall be your servant; and whoever wishes to be first among you shall be slave of all."*

All followers of Christ who serve in a leadership capacity must humbly encourage others, want the best for them, and help empower them. There is no place for the proud or power-hungry. It is no accident that the person God chose to lead the children of Israel out of Egyptian captivity was identified as "Moses, my servant," not "Moses, my leader."

The leader's attitude toward others

Most business leaders tend to focus on their tasks, their own success, and the bottom line. Frequently unkind to subordinates, they often take credit for the accomplishments of those under their authority.

Juan Gonzales's father was a successful businessman who ruled his staff with an iron fist. He groomed Juan to take over the family business and often counseled him, "Let the employees know who's the boss. Be tough. Be hard when you're dealing with them."

When his father retired, Juan became CEO and followed his advice. Later Juan became concerned that customer service was a growing problem since the company had earned the reputation of treating customers rudely. He hired a consultant to discover the cause.

After dozens of interviews, the consultant shared his conclusion with Juan: "*You* are the problem! The way you treat your employees is the way they are treating your customers."

Philippians 2:3-4 tells us how we should view others. It says, *"Do nothing from selfishness or empty conceit, but with humility of mind regard one another as more important than yourselves; do not merely look out for your own personal interests, but also for the interests of others."* These verses contain three radical commands that are impossible to obey apart from yielding to the Lord. Carefully study them.

- *"Do nothing from selfishness or empty conceit."* We are to do absolutely **nothing** from selfishness or because of pride.

- *"but with humility of mind regard one another as more important than yourselves."* We are to think of **everyone** as more important than ourselves.

- *"do not merely look out for your own personal interests, but also for the interests of others."* We are not to focus exclusively on doing what is important to us, but also factor in how we can serve the interests of **others**.

With this passage as the standard, how would you rate yourself as a leader (on a scale of 1-10, with 10 being the best) who thinks others as more important than yourself? If you need to improve in this area, what will you do?

NINE

Spiritual Disciples

Jesus' first words to his disciples were, *"Follow Me"* (Matthew 4:19), and his last words to Peter were also *"Follow Me"* (John 21:22). He wants us to follow Him in every area of life, including business, and to make more Christ-followers however we can. Nothing is more important for the business leader than to grow closer to Christ. The only way to grow is to practice spiritual disciplines.

Tom Landry, former coach of the Dallas Cowboys, said, "The job of a football coach is to make men do what they don't want to do in order to achieve what they've always wanted to be." Think of spiritual disciplines as spiritual exercises. To go to your favorite place for prayer, for example, is like going to a gym to exercise.

Just as in athletics, there is discipline involved in Christian growth. How rapidly a person grows spiritually depends upon this discipline. The Apostle Paul instructed his protégé Timothy to *"Discipline yourself for the purpose of godliness"* (1 Timothy 4:7). This was a command, not a suggestion.

The disciplines of Bible study, prayer, and reading outstanding Christian books are meant to lead somewhere: to a closer relationship with Christ. When we remember that goal, the disciplines become a delight instead of drudgery. It's crucial to keep the big picture in mind: the reason to practice spiritual disciplines is not to check another item off our "to do" list; it's to grow closer to Christ.

Bible Reading

No spiritual discipline is more important than investing time in God's Word. There is simply no healthy Christian life apart from this commitment. In the Bible, God tells us about Himself. Only in the Scriptures do we find how to live in a way that pleases God and, as a byproduct, truly fulfills us.

When Jesus asked people about their understanding of the Scriptures, he often began with the words, "Have you not read?" He assumed that those claiming to be the people of God would have read the Word of God. Unfortunately, this is often not the case. A recent survey found that only 18 percent of followers of Christ read the Bible every day, and 23 percent never read it.

Here are four suggestions for consistent success in Bible reading:

1. **Find the time.** Perhaps one of the main reasons Christians never read through the entire Bible is its sheer length. Do you realize that tape-recorded readings of the Bible have proved that you can read through the entire Bible in 71 hours? In no more than 15 minutes a day you can read through the Bible in a year's time. Try to make it the same time every day.

2. **Find a Bible-reading plan.** It's no wonder that those who simply open the Bible at random each day soon drop the discipline. There are effective Bible-reading plans available at Christian bookstores and online. *YouVersion* is an outstanding online tool. It is a free app that contains hundreds of different translations and versions of the Bible and different plans to help you in your study of God's word.

3. **Find one phrase or verse to meditate on each time you read.** Take a few moments to think deeply about it for a few moments. This will

change your life. The Lord commanded Joshua, *"This book of the law shall not depart from your mouth, but you shall meditate on it day and night, so that you may be careful to do according to all that is written in it; for then . . . you will have success"* (Joshua 1:8). You may be thinking, "That's great for Joshua, but I've got a company to run! I can't think about the Bible all day long. I've got decisions to make. It just isn't practical."

Let me assure you that meditation is the most practical thing in the world. Joshua didn't just sit around all day thinking about the Scriptures. He had two million people to manage. Joshua was as busy, if not busier, than you will ever be. So how does a busy person meditate on the Bible? Read through a portion of the Bible and when a verse grabs you, jot it down, then take it with you, reviewing it at different times during the day.

4. **Find a Bible study.** Most of us will be more consistent if we become involved in a Bible study. We need the encouragement and account-ability of a group. And one of the greatest benefits of a group is the development of close relationships with others who are seeking to know the Lord better.

Prayer

If prayer could have been unnecessary for anyone, surely it would have been Jesus Christ, the sinless Son of God.

But it wasn't "unnecessary" to Jesus at all.

If fact, it was His lifeblood.

It was not only a frequent theme in His teaching, it was the dominant habit of His life. "[Jesus] *spent the whole night in prayer to God"* (Luke 6:12). He often rose before daylight to pray: *"In the early morning, while it was still dark, Jesus got up, left the house and went away to a secluded place, and was praying there"* (Mark 1:35).

Even in the midst of His busy public ministry, the Lord consistently spent time alone with His heavenly Father. *"But Jesus often withdrew to lonely places and prayed"* (Luke 5:16, NIV). Jesus is our supreme example for prayer.

Throughout history, godly leaders have recognized the importance of prayer. Samuel Chadwick said, "The one concern of the devil is to keep Christians from praying. He fears nothing from our prayerless work, prayerless religion. He laughs at our toil, he mocks our wisdom, but he trembles when we pray." And it was John Wesley's conviction that "God does nothing but in answer to prayer."

As with reading the Bible, most of us will be more consistent if we establish a regular time in our daily schedule to pray. It's also helpful to establish a list of people and circumstances for which to pray. I have a daily prayer list that takes about 15 minutes to pray through. It includes members of my family, friends, the needs of Compass's staff, and other important situations.

The reason to practice spiritual disciplines is not to check another item off our "to do" list; it's to grow closer to Christ.

Reading Christian Books

The person who desires to grow spiritually should read consistently. Unfortunately, the habit of reading solid Christian literature is rare. Because there are so many books available today, it's important to be selective in what you read. We can afford to read only the best, the ones that will be the most helpful to us.

Reading should involve not only scanning the words but also meditating on the thoughts they express. Charles H. Spurgeon counseled his students: "Master the books you have. Read them thoroughly. Read and reread them. Let them go into your very self. Peruse a good book several times and make notes and analyses of it. You will be is more affected by one book thoroughly mastered than by twenty books merely skimmed."

In reading, let your motto be "much, not many." Sir Francis Bacon's famous rule for reading was: "Read not to contradict or confute, nor to believe and take for granted, but to weigh and consider. Some books are to be tested, others to be swallowed, and some few to be chewed and digested."

Prioritize Time

Leaders should prioritize their time. Just as we should budget to avoid impulse spending, so leaders should plan the use of their time to prevent squandering it. Ephesians 5:16 says, *"Make . . . the most of your time."*

An effective way to manage time is to use a prioritized To-Do list. Start by making a list of the items that you would like to accomplish on a given day. Then identify those which *must* be done today, and put an "A" next to each one. Then put a "B" beside the remaining items that should be done very soon. The remaining activities get a "C".

Now examine the A items and choose the most important item that must be done today—and place a "1" next to it, making that A1. Then choose the next most important, which becomes A2, and so on through the A's, B's, and C's. You now have prioritized what you need to do today, starting with A1.

To-Do list October 7

A1 – Execute software contract

A2 – Call Nancy Smith

A3 – Meet with VP of Marketing

B1 – Read the WSJ report

B2 – Call Brad Pierce

C1 – Draft Jones sales agreement

Yes, I realize this is almost childishly simple. But you would be surprised how much time all of us tend to waste when we find ourselves with a "blank slate" in the morning. Sometimes we look back on a day that has slipped through our fingers and ask ourselves, "What in the world did I accomplish today." The modest, easily-implemented technique I just mentioned will help you to maximize your time and accomplish more of your priorities and spiritual disciplines.

Sexual Purity

John was the president of a multi-billion dollar subsidiary of one of the best known companies in the world. As an outspoken follower of Christ, he was influencing many people for the Lord. However, he had developed the habit of traveling alone with attractive female colleagues. In time, he became sexually involved with one of these women, and after a very public and nasty divorce, they were married. John ultimately lost his marriage, his job, his influence for Christ, and the respect of his family.

None of us are exempt from the challenge of sexual temptation. (And the moment you *think* you are, is the moment you should begin to worry.) The key is to build what I call "guardrails," to keep you from crossing over into this temptation. For example, I've adopted Billy Graham's practice of never being alone with a member of the opposite sex who isn't a family member. So in the office, car, or over a meal, I am *never* alone with a woman other than Bev.

> *"This book of the law shall not depart from your mouth, but you shall meditate on it day and night, so that you may be careful to do according to all that is written in it; for then . . . you will have success"*
> (Joshua 1:8).

Is this inconvenient? Yes, it is.

Sometimes awkward? Absolutely.

But it's worth it!

I've made some other sexual guardrail decisions as well. Each week I answer my accountability partner Tim Manor's question, "Are you attracted to a woman other than Bev?" Bev also has my calendar, and I do not send an email or text to a female without copying her. This sends the message that we are serious about keeping our marriage strong.

Decades ago I committed to never look lustfully at another woman. If I'm driving and see an attractive woman out of the corner of my eye, I remind myself, *Don't look to the left or the right, keep your eyes straight ahead.*

So, here's my suggestion: If there is a provocative scene on the tube, change the channel or turn it off. If you've got a problem with internet pornography, get rid of the computer—or install software that will block porn.

It is critical for the leader to do whatever it takes to set up guardrails to maintain sexual purity. Hebrews 13:4 bluntly tells us, *"Marriage should be honored by all, and the marriage bed kept pure, for God will judge the adulterer and all the sexually immoral."*

Remember, nothing is more important for the business leader than to grow closer to Christ. It will help you begin these disciplines if you complete plan on the next page—and it will help you to *maintain* these disciplines if you invite someone to hold you accountable. If you are married, discuss these with your spouse. It is much easier to practice these if your mate participates.

Your Spiritual Disciplines Plan

1. *Bible study*

How often—

Select the Bible or Bible study program—

2. *Prayer*

How often and how much time—

Location—

Draft a list of people and things for which to pray—

3. *Reading Christian books*

How often—

How much time—

I will read the following books—

TEN

Honesty

Dave Palmer's company invested hundreds of thousands of dollars in a complex proposal to develop a sophisticated software system for one of the largest cities in America. In the process of their research, however, his staff discovered that other companies competing for the project had been holding private, illegal discussions with the city commissioners who were going to award the project.

When Dave's staff asked his permission to initiate similar discussions with the commissioners, David responded without hesitation.

"No," he said. "Under no circumstances will we do something like that. I'd rather lose ten times the money we've invested in the proposal than do anything that would compromise our integrity!" As it turned out, Palmer Software lost the competition, but Dave's honesty gained the respect of his employees —and influenced some of them to consider Christ as their Savior.

There are hundreds of verses in the Bible that communicate the Lord's desire for us to be completely honest. Proverbs 20:23 reads, *"The Lord loathes all cheating and dishonesty"* (TLB). And Proverbs 12:22 says, *"Lying lips are an abomination to the LORD."* Proverbs 6:16-17 adds,

"The LORD hates . . . a lying tongue."

Truthfulness is one of God's attributes.

In fact, Jesus IS the truth.

He said, *"I am . . . the truth"* (John 14:6), and He commands us to reflect His honest and holy character. The Apostle Peter wrote: *"Be holy yourselves also in all your behavior; because it is written, 'You shall be holy, for I am holy'"* (1 Peter 1:15-16).

As the very embodiment of truth, Jesus is holy, and no lie can be found in Him. And this is the very One who lives within you! When we submit to Christ, allowing Him to live His life through us, we are going to be absolutely honest business leaders.

Have you ever thought about this? When we are dishonest we act as though the living God didn't even exist! Don't we believe that He is present with us and able to provide for our needs even though He has promised to do so? When we decide to take things into our own hands and do them in our own dishonest way, we act as if God is incapable of discovering our dishonesty and that He is powerless to discipline us. If we really believe God will discipline us, then we won't even consider acting in a dishonest way.

"You shall not steal, nor deal falsely, nor lie to one another"
(*Leviticus 19:11*).

Honest behavior is often an issue of faith. An honest decision may look foolish in light of what we can see, but the godly person knows that Jesus Christ is alive even though He is invisible to us. Every honest decision strengthens our faith in the living God and helps us grow into a closer relationship with Christ. However, if we choose to be dishonest, we essentially deny our Lord and violate the greatest commandment. *"You shall love the Lord your God with all your heart, and with all your soul, and will all your mind"* (Matthew 22:37). It is impossible to love God like this if, at the same time, we are dishonest and act as if He does not exist.

Honesty of Leaders

The Lord is especially concerned with the honesty of leaders, because they exercise such strong influence over those whom they employ. The owner of a trucking business began wearing cowboy boots to work. Within six months, all the men in his office were in boots. He suddenly changed to a traditional business shoe, and six months later all the men traded their boots for business shoes.

In a similar way, a dishonest leader produces dishonest followers. *"If a ruler pays attention to falsehood, all his ministers become wicked"* (Proverbs 29:12). Leaders in business must set the example of honesty before they can expect those under their authority to do the same.

The president of a large international construction company was asked why her company did not work in countries where bribes and graft were a way of life. She responded, "We never build in those countries, no matter how profitable the project may appear, because we can't afford to. If our employees know we are acting dishonestly, they will eventually become thieves. Their dishonesty will ultimately cost us more than we could ever earn on a project."

> *The Lord is especially concerned with the honesty of leaders, because they exercise such strong influence over those whom they employ.*

There are several other reasons why leaders should be completely honest.

Dishonest gain will be taken from us.

Our heavenly Father ultimately will not allow us to keep anything we have acquired dishonestly. Proverbs 13:11 reads, *"Wealth obtained by fraud dwindles."* Think about this for a moment: If you are a parent and one of your children steals something, do you allow the child to keep it? Of course not. You require your child to return the item, because his or her character would be damaged by keeping stolen property. Not only do you insist on its return, you usually want the child to experience enough discomfort to produce a lasting impression. For instance, you might have the child confess the theft and ask forgiveness from the store manager.

When our heavenly Father lovingly disciplines us, he usually does it in such a way that we won't soon forget.

We cannot practice dishonesty and love our neighbor.

The Lord also demands absolute honesty because dishonest behavior violates the second commandment, *"You shall love your neighbor as yourself"* (Mark 12:31). Romans 13:9-10 reads, *"If you love your neighbor as much as you love yourself you will not want to harm or cheat him, or kill him or steal from him . . . love does no wrong to anyone"* (TLB).

We must understand that when we act dishonestly, we are stealing from another person. We may rationalize that it's only a "faceless" business or the government suffering the loss, but that isn't true, is it? Ultimately, we are stealing from people, whether it is the business owner or taxpayers. It is just as if we took the money from their wallets. Dishonesty always injures people; no matter how we might try to deceive ourselves, the victim is always a person.

> ***We must understand that when we act dishonestly, we are stealing from another person. It's just as if we took the money from their wallets.***

Honesty provides credibility to influence others for Christ

Another reason our Lord demands absolute honesty in the way we operate our business is to demonstrate the reality of Jesus Christ to those around us.

I once told my neighbor, Jim, how he could come to know Christ as his personal Savior. Jim became angry and snarled, "Well, I know a business-man who goes to church and talks a lot about Jesus, but watch out if you ever get in a business deal with him! He'd cheat his own grandmother! If that's what it means to be a Christian, I don't want any part of it!"

Our actions speak louder than our words. Scripture says to *"Prove yourselves to be blameless and innocent, children of God above reproach in the midst of a crooked and perverse generation, among whom you appear as lights in the world"* (Philippians 2:15). Our honesty can influence people for Jesus Christ.

For months, Ed Rahill had been trying to sell a business vehicle because cash flow was tight. Finally, an interested buyer decided to purchase it—but at the last moment threw in a condition. The prospective purchaser said, "I'll buy it, but only if you don't report the full sale price, so I won't have to pay all the sales tax."

Ed was tempted to agree—for a moment. Then he shook his head and responded, "Sorry. I can't do that, because Jesus Christ is my Lord." Ed later said, "You should have witnessed the buyer's reaction. He almost went into shock! Then an interesting thing happened. His attitude completely changed. Not only did he purchase the vehicle, but rarely have I seen anyone as open to the truth about knowing Jesus Christ in a personal way."

Ed acted honestly, even though it could have cost him money he really needed. In the process, he demonstrated to this individual the reality of a personal faith in Jesus Christ. By acting the way he did, Ed lived out the truth of Philippians 2:15-16: *"Prove yourselves to be blameless and innocent, children of God above reproach in the midst of a crooked and perverse generation, among whom you appear as lights in the world..."*

Bribes

A bribe is anything given to influence a person to do something illegal or wrong. The taking of bribes is clearly prohibited in the Bible: *"You shall not take a bribe, for a bribe blinds the clear-sighted and subverts the cause of the just"* (Exodus 23:8). If a leader takes bribes, it jeopardizes the entire business. Proverbs 29:4 says it this way, *"The king gives stability to the land by justice, but a man who takes bribes overthrows it."*

What to Do When Dishonesty Creeps in

What do we do if we have sold or acquired anything dishonestly? The Bible is clear: we must make restitution. *"Then it shall be, when he sins and becomes guilty, that he shall restore what he took by robbery . . . or anything about which he swore falsely; he shall make restitution for it in full and add to it one-fifth more. He shall give it to the one to whom it belongs"* (Leviticus 6:4-5).

Restitution is a tangible expression of repentance and an effort to correct a wrong. Zaccheus is a good example of fulfilling this principle. He promised Jesus, *"If I have defrauded anyone of anything, I will give back four times as much"* (Luke 19:8).

Blessings and Curses

Listed below are some of the blessings the Lord has promised for the honest—and some of the curses reserved for the dishonest. Read these slowly, asking God to use them to motivate you to a life of honesty.

Blessings for the Honest

- Blessing of a closer relationship with the Lord. *"For the crooked man is an abomination to the LORD; but He is intimate with the upright"* (Proverbs 3:32).

- Blessings on the family. *"A righteous man who walks in his integrity—how blessed are his sons after him"* (Proverbs 20:7).

- Blessings of life. *"Truthful lips will be established forever, but a lying tongue is only for a moment"* (Proverbs 12:19).

- Blessings of prosperity. *"Great wealth is in the house of the righteous, but trouble is in the income of the wicked"* (Proverbs 15:6).

Curses Reserved for the Dishonest

- Curse of alienation from God. *"For the crooked man is an abomination to the LORD"* (Proverbs 3:32).

- Curse on the family. *"He who profits illicitly troubles his own house, but he who hates bribes will live"* (Proverbs 15:27).

- Curse of death. *"The acquisition of treasures by a lying tongue is a fleeting vapor, the pursuit of death"* (Proverbs 21:6).

- Curse of poverty. *"Wealth obtained by fraud dwindles"* (Proverbs 13:11).

Honesty is Big to God

We tend to underestimate how important honesty is to the Lord. Jeremiah 5:1 says, *"Go up and down the streets of Jerusalem and look around and consider, search through her squares. If you can find but one person who deals honestly and seeks the truth, I will forgive the city."*

Think about this. The future of an entire city hung in the balance, and what was the Lord looking for before executing judgment on it?

Just one honest person.

I believe the same is true for your business. The Lord is still seeking honest people. Are you willing to be that one person in your business? Are you willing to be completely honest in even the smallest matters? If you are that person, you may not be noticed by other people, but you will please an audience of One. The One who really matters—the Lord Jesus Christ.

ELEVEN

Empowering Others

Building trust in followers is crucial for a godly leader. You can't have a great business without great trust. Each of us has what I call a *Trust Account.* Just as with a bank account, a leader can make deposits and withdrawals from an employee's trust account. There are no shortcuts to filling another person's trust account. Trust must be earned, and if it's violated, it often takes a long time to recover.

Building trust in a company led by followers of Christ begins with people realizing that the leader is close to the Lord and has a vibrant prayer life. People also look for a leader who consistently communicates and has character and competence. The absence of any of these creates insecurity and distrust among followers. Let's examine the life of Nehemiah, who is an outstanding example of a trusted leader.

Nehemiah communicated a vision that would help people, and he told of how the Lord granted him favor with the king to provide the supplies to accomplish it. *"I [Nehemiah] said to the king, 'If it please the king, let letters be given me . . . to Asaph the keeper of the king's forest, that he may give me timber . . . for the wall of the city.' And the king granted them to me because the good hand of my God was on me . . . I told them* [citizens of Jerusalem] *how the hand of my God had been favorable to me and also about the king's words which he had spoken to me. Then, they said, 'Let us arise and build.' So they put their hands to the good work"* (Nehemiah 2:7-8, 18).

Nehemiah also set the example of being a hard worker. *"All of us returned to the wall, each one to his work . . . I also applied myself to the work on the wall"* (Nehemiah 5:15-16). Lastly, Nehemiah refused to exploit people; rather, he was generous in meeting their needs. *"From the day that I was appointed to be their governor . . . for twelve years, neither I nor my kinsmen have eaten the governor's food allowance. But the former governors laid burdens on the people and took from them bread and wine besides* [taxes] *. . . But I did not do so because of the fear of God . . . I did not demand the governor's food allowance, because the servitude was heavy on this people"* (Nehemiah 5:14-15, 18).

> **A business may have superb products, systems, and technology, with a strong brand in the marketplace. Yet without the amazing capacity of the right people, the business will never achieve its potential.**

Empowering People

A business may have superb products, systems, and technology, with a strong brand in the marketplace. Yet without the amazing capacity of the right people, the business will never achieve its potential.

People are able to work through complex situations, guiding and motivating others. They adapt to new challenges and situations. We need people. While many businesses fall into the trap of treating people as an *expense,* far better to remember that the right people are an *investment,* providing the greatest return possible.

Let's explore how to maximize the potential of people in your business by learning how to empower them.

Someone once said, "It's better to get ten people to do the work than to do the work of ten people!" In other words, delegate! One of the best examples of delegation in the Bible is that of Jethro's advice to his son-in-law Moses. Under the courageous leadership of Moses, about two million refugees escaped their slavery in Egypt to start a new nation. Once they were on their journey, Moses became the sole judge adjudicating all the conflicts that arose. *"Moses sat to judge the people, and the people stood about Moses from the morning until the evening"* (Exodus 18:13).

That made for a very long day, and Jethro immediately concluded that Moses wouldn't be able to maintain such a killer schedule indefinitely. Speaking with the kind bluntness of a father-in-law, he told Moses, *"What you are doing is not good. You and these people who come to you will only wear yourselves out. The work is too heavy for you; you cannot handle it alone"* (Exodus 18:17-18, NIV).

Surround yourself with capable people, give them responsibility, measure their productivity, and reward those who have been faithful with even more responsibility.

There are limits to how hard and long you can work. You can't push yourself 24/7 without eventually compromising your health, your ability to make wise decisions, your family, and your career. It also will discourage others with whom you work.

Jethro realized Moses was uniquely qualified to do certain things that only he could do. He had to delegate all other tasks. *"I [Jethro] will give you counsel, and God be with you. You be the people's representative before God, and you bring the disputes to God. Then teach them the statutes and the laws, and make known to them the way in which they are to walk and the work they are to do"* (Exodus 18:19-20).

Moses needed to offload the tasks that others could do so he could focus on those things that only he could do. The same is true for you. Dawson Trotman, the founder of the Navigators, said, "Never do anything of importance that others can do or will do when there is so much of importance to do that others cannot do or will not do." Where do you add the most value in your business? What are you uniquely capable of doing? How can you delegate the rest?

Select qualified leaders and give them responsibility and authority

Jethro didn't just leave Moses with a good theory; he told him how to implement a system. *"Select out of all the people able men who fear God, men of truth, those who hate dishonest gain"* (Exodus 18:21, NIV). Notice that Jethro's criteria for choosing leaders focused on their character—men who fear God, men of truth, those who hate dishonest gain. People can gain knowledge and experience, and they can learn skills and develop their gifts, but you must start with a foundation of godly character. When competent subordinates have character, it is much easier to trust them and to delegate.

Jethro also understood that a leader's span of control was limited. He established a simple organizational structure with different levels of responsibility. *"Appoint them as officials over thousands, hundreds, fifties, and tens."* (Exodus 18:21, NIV). Then, Jethro advocated that Moses manage by exception: *"Have them serve as judges for the people at all times, but have them bring every difficult case to you; the simple cases they can decide themselves. That will make your load lighter, because they will share it with you"* (Exodus 18:22, NIV).

This isn't rocket science. Nor is it a bureaucracy. These management levels weren't designed to impede decision making but to facilitate it. The key is in giving your people authority.

But what if they make mistakes?

Trust me, they will. Get over it. This is part of the price you pay to develop leaders.

Jethro concluded his advice for Moses by observing, *"If you do this and God so commands, you will be able to stand the strain, and all these people will go home satisfied."* He promised two benefits: Moses wouldn't burn out, and the people would be content. Do those sound like benefits you need more of: less stress and more peace at work?

Let's face it, it can be hard to give up control and appoint others to do a task. Sometimes this is an issue of our pride when we're convinced that no one else can do the job as well as we can. Surround yourself with capable people, give them responsibility, measure their productivity, and reward those who have been faithful with even more responsibility.

Communication

Building the tower of Babel illustrates the importance of good communication. The story begins at a time when everyone speaks the same language. The Lord observed: *"If as one people speaking the same language they have begun to do this* [build the tower], *then nothing they plan to do will be impossible for them"* (Genesis 11:6, NIV).

In a similar way, when a business is committed to good communication and a common goal, then *"nothing they plan to do will be impossible for them"*—as long as it is within the will of God. Since building the tower wasn't what the Lord wanted, He stopped construction simply by disrupting their ability to communicate. *"Come, let us go down and confuse their language so they will not understand each other"* (Genesis 11:7, NIV).

The biggest step most us can take to upgrade our communication is to improve our listening skills. We must give undivided attention—and that takes some effort! Get away from the phone, pager, e-mail, texts, and other distractions. If your iPhone keeps beeping, buzzing, or chirping, *turn it off.* Give your team member eye contact, and resist "cutting to the chase" or jumping in with a quick solution to what you perceive the problem to be. Respectful listening is the key to understanding employees' feelings and needs.

When a leader *really* listens to you, you feel cared for and understood, which is the foundation for cooperation in problem solving. Many conflicts result from our mistaken assumptions about what others really mean. It's crucial to ask as many questions as necessary to help you understand. Asking questions demonstrates you care and want to understand their concerns. It is especially important for the godly leader to listen to employee complaints. *"If I have despised the claim of my . . .* [employees] *when they filed a complaint against me, what then could I do when God arises? And when He calls me to account, what will I answer Him?"* (Job 31:13-15). When a complaint is legitimate, employers should take appropriate steps to solve the problem.

> *The biggest step most us can take to upgrade our communication is to improve our listening skills.*

Jesus said, *"Every . . . household divided against itself will not stand"* (Matthew 12:25, NIV). In a similar way, every business divided against itself will not achieve optimal results. The key for not being divided is to know what God says about business and to communicate well with one another. The leader must communicate in an honest, straightforward way that is not intended to manipulate people. Allow subordinates to express their real feelings without fear of retribution. And don't try to solve major conflicts over the phone or via email. Neither of these allows you to observe each other's body language, which is an irreplaceable component of meaningful communication.

Regular Communication.

A weekly, or even daily, scheduled time for communication is vital because it establishes the habit of regular conversations when there is no crisis. Many businesspeople don't begin a conversation unless a significant problem has surfaced and the panic button has already been punched. Tension can reach the boiling point in a hurry when blame and defensiveness take over. But if you communicate regularly and are current on the issues facing the business, it's much easier to resolve an unexpected problem.

Dave Rae was hired by Apple Canada as Vice President of Operations and within a year was promoted to President. At the time he assumed the role, Apple Canada's annual sales were $88 million, and the corporate mandate was to grow sales.

Dave believed that exponential sales growth would happen only by growing his staff through a culture of values and empowerment. Although Apple had established nine corporate values, they were virtually unknown in Canada. Dave's challenge was to delegate and align his staff by bringing the values to life.

Initially, he focused on practicing the values that were crucial: teamwork, innovation, and collaboration. Dave's leaders established a quarterly celebration and rewarded those who were living the values. His staff started looking for these values in other team members, and the culture of Apple Canada changed.

Leading a company based on values and delegation paid off. People became more motivated and grew in their commitment to serve one another and the customer. The company experienced rapid sales growth without adding people.

When the Department of Education ordered $10 million of computers, it was the largest single sale in the company history in Canada. However, three months later, when Apple reduced the price of these computers by 10 percent, the government demanded a $1 million rebate or threatened that they would return the computers.

Dave and his team faced a challenging situation. Price decreases in the industry were common, and it wasn't the industry norm to extend rebates. As a team, they examined the facts: They had not compromised a single value in the transaction. Apple corporate wanted to keep the profit and didn't want to set a precedent for future price reduction rebates. On the other hand, they didn't want to lose this sale and future business.

Dave and his team felt their values would guide them to a wise decision. After listening to the customer, to Apple corporate, and their team members, they collectively decided to offer the Department of Education a $1 million voucher on future sales.

Dave and his team valued the customer by listening and by finding a creative solution. They valued Apple by not returning the profit or losing the customer. The team felt enormously valued as they were part of suggesting the creative solution. Oh, and by the way, they were excited to participate in the profit sharing from the sale.

Next year, the Department of Education placed another order for $10 million and applied the voucher to the purchase. Values, communication, and empowerment pay dividends!

TWELVE

Human Resources

E ric Menendez and Dave Palmer sat at a small table in the coffee shop. After a bit of small talk, Eric zoomed in on what was really troubling him.

"I need to pick your brain a little, Dave. How in the world do you make good hiring decisions? I opened my printing company three years ago, and I always seem to hire the wrong people. They end up performing poorly and chewing up too much of my time, trying to straighten them out. Then—within a year or so—they end up leaving anyway!"

"I had the same problem when I first started in business," Dave replied. "What's your process for hiring?"

"I advertise online and select the best candidate from those who apply," Eric answered. "I know what experience is necessary for the job. And when I find someone who's had at least a years' experience in the printing business, I hire them."

"Do you check references?" David asked. "And what about running background checks and personality assessments?"

"I just don't have the time or money for that," Eric replied. "Only the big guys can afford to do stuff like that."

"That's not true," Dave responded. "At Palmer Software we do those things— because it's always cheaper to hire the right people the first time."

Here's how you can improve your hiring decisions.

Create a business that attracts qualified candidates.

Potential employees are interested in companies that have good reputations, pay a fair wage, and care for their staff. These businesses usually can be selective when hiring because they often have more applicants than openings. Evaluate your business. Are your employees encouraged, respected, and compensated fairly? If so, they will spread this news by word of mouth and social media.

Create clear expectations.

One of the most important steps when hiring is to create a written job description that clearly addresses the duties and expectations of the position and the skills and experience needed to be successful. This increases your likelihood of hiring the right person, and it pleases the Lord that you care enough for potential employees to help them evaluate whether they are well suited for job.

The best place to start a search to fill a position is within your own organization. Whenever possible, post open positions within the company before going public. You will know the competencies and potential of those already working for you. And promoting from within can motivate existing staff.

If there are no qualified candidates in the business, employee referrals are an excellent place to search. Your employees know the company and are able to recommend potential hires that would be a good fit for its culture.

Gather sufficient information.

Too many leaders trust their initial gut instincts without really getting to know a candidate. A survey discovered that the average time for a leader to make a hiring decision in an interview is *4.3 minutes*! That's barely enough time to break the ice, let alone make a hiring decision.

Establish an interviewing process that always includes several of your staff conducting an interview with a prospective employee. This yields a more accurate assessment of the candidate than one interview alone. One extremely successful fast food chain interviews candidates applying for positions in their home office ten times!

We significantly improved the quality of our executive assistants when we asked Marcia Moore and our other best-performing executive assistants to interview candidates when there was an opening for this position. They knew exactly what it would take to fit into our culture and function at a high level. Marcia and her peers felt affirmed and empowered, so they were careful to recommend only the best qualified applicants. But it didn't stop there. They also took the initiative to begin a mentoring program for the new hires.

> *Establish an interviewing process that always includes several of your staff conducting an interview with a prospective employee. This yields a more accurate assessment of the candidate than one interview alone.*

Interviews over a meal or any casual setting can be especially helpful as the candidates are more relaxed and reveal more of their natural personalities. The most accurate feedback is obtained when standardized interview questions are used for all applicants. These interviews are more reliable—and also have the benefit of being more legally defensible.

Statistically validated personality and aptitude assessment tools are also very helpful, and will help you understand your candidates more thoroughly. Finally, conduct a drug test and criminal background check, examine their credit report, and check the applicant's references.

Use a trial period.

Establishing a 90-day trial for new hires provides you the opportunity to evaluate compatibility and job performance. Let's face it, no matter how effective the hiring process, it's easy to make a mistake. New employees and the business both benefit if you realize they will not succeed in the job and you sever employment during the trial period.

Be patient.

Practice patience when making a hiring decision. This can be difficult and even stressful when you have a vacancy that must be filled soon. You may be tempted to quickly hire a mediocre performer to solve a short-term problem…but you also may regret it!

In his book, *Good to Great,* Jim Collins uses the word picture of "getting the right people on the bus, and getting the people in the right seats on the bus." In other words, hire the right people and place them in the role for which they are best suited.

> *In his book, Good to Great, Jim Collins uses the word picture of "getting the right people on the bus, and getting the people in the right seats on the bus." In other words, hire the right people and place them in the role for which they are best suited.*

Finally, and most importantly, practice patience by bringing your hiring decisions before the Lord in prayer. Nothing can replace the wisdom of the *"Wonderful Counselor"* (Isaiah 9:6) who knows the best person for the job.

Developing Talent

Just as wise parents identify the interests and abilities of their children and create opportunities for them to develop these God-given talents, leaders should do the same with their employees.

Employee development has been a cornerstone of building strong organizations for millennia. In 600 BC, King Nebuchadnezzar chose young leaders from the captives of Israel who had *"aptitude for every kind of learning, well informed, quick to understand, and qualified to serve in the king's palace"* (Daniel 1:4, NIV) He trained them for three years before engaging them in his service. During this training and development period, the king monitored their progress and found Daniel, Shadrach, Meshach, and Abednego to be ten times better than any of the others. These four godly men would eventually help rule the kingdom, and bring God's blessing on the realm.

We recommend that leaders meet with their direct reports and create a "Development Plan" to capitalize on employees' strengths. Research has discovered that employee effectiveness is amplified as it zeroes in on *improving strengths* rather than simply addressing weaknesses.

Which would you choose, an employee who progressed to moderately competent in an area of weakness, or an employee who improved from good to superstar in an area of strength?

The most important filter to utilize when considering whether to promote an employee is found in Matthew 25:21. *"His master said, 'Well done, good and faithful servant! You have been faithful with a few things; I will put you in charge of many things"* (NIV). Have the candidates been faithful in their current position? If not, don't count on them suddenly developing faithfulness in their greater responsibilities.

In most instances, promotions should be treated similarly to a new hire. Competencies for the open job should be clearly defined and the position posted internally even if you have identified a candidate that you feel is a good fit for the position. This reduces the possibility of being perceived as playing favorites.

Termination of Employment

One of the most difficult responsibilities of a godly leader is terminating an employee. There are different reasons for dismissing an employee: dishonesty, laziness, disobedience, or the inability to perform the job satisfactorily. Other times businesses are forced to reduce the number of staff simply to survive. Some of the most difficult situations are dealing with a cooperative but incompetent employee or an extraordinarily productive employee who is violating the values of the company.

Let's examine the process a leader should use before terminating an employee.

1. Create clear expectations of work performance using a written job description and by carefully communicating the company's values.

2. Review job performance regularly and communicate any dissatisfaction promptly and in writing. Too often, leaders allow personnel problems to go unchecked until they reach the boiling point; then they unload on an employee who should have been told long before. Communicate early, often, and clearly.

3. Provide an opportunity to correct unsatisfactory performance. Unless employees are guilty of stealing or some other offense punishable by immediate termination, first give them an opportunity to change. Begin a trial period and tell them the purpose of the trial: Either shape up or you will have to ship out. Describe their shortcomings and requirements of the trial period in writing and document it in their personnel file.

A Leader's Attitude

Sometimes a leader must dismiss an employee who has betrayed trust or stolen company property. In these circumstances, it's easy to be angry and harsh during the firing process.

That, however, is not business God's way.

Instead, let passages like these govern your behavior: *"Do not let kindness and truth leave you"* (Proverbs 3:3). *"[Speak] the truth in love"* (Ephesians 4:15). We can be direct about the reason for the termination and express our disappointment, yet we are to communicate it in a winsome way. How we act in these emotional situations can be a testimony of the reality of Christ in our lives.

The most important filter to utilize when considering whether to promote an employee is found in Matthew 25:21. "His master said, 'Well done, good and faithful servant! You have been faithful with a few things; I will put you in charge of many things."

Employee Pay

Godly leaders should care for their staff in a way that positively impacts their lives and honors God. This involves creating an environment where everyone is valued for their unique abilities and employees are compensated fairly. The Lord is particularly concerned about employers paying a fair wage.

Consider these passages:

- *"So I will come to put you on trial. I will be quick to testify against . . . those who defraud laborers of their wages . . . says the LORD Almighty"* (Malachi 3:5, NIV).
- *"Do not take advantage of a hired worker who is poor and needy"* (Deuteronomy 24:14, NIV).

What does it mean to "pay people fairly"? It means leaders should do their homework and understand the value of the position and the experience and proficiency of an employee. It means providing appropriate benefits such as health insurance, retirement plans, and paid vacations. Whenever possible, institute a bonus program in which employees share in the profitability of the company and are rewarded for outstanding performance.

Startups and Entrepreneurs

Some businesses are started by an entrepreneur who has a vision to operate it for God's glory. Too many give ownership in the company to executives or those investing capital in the company. Some even relinquish a majority of the company and lose control of it.

In my experience, this is usually a mistake—a tragic mistake. The Lord has entrusted a vision to a particular person, and if control of the business is lost or diluted, its values and purpose are often compromised. Instead, I recommend compensating key leaders and investors from profits as if they had an ownership interest in the company, but for the founder to retain a strong majority of the ownership—in face, as much ownership as possible. This greatly simplifies ultimate decision making and helps avoid a host of problems.

Business Plan

LEADERSHIP PLAN

Board of Directors/Trustees

Job description:

_____

_____

_____

Criteria for selection (experience, expertise, loyalty, etc.):

_____

_____

_____

Responsibilities:

_____

_____

_____

Plan to effectively communicate with the Board:

_____

_____

_____

Leadership Team

Who are the members of your leadership team? Describe the role of each member.

_____

_____

_____

Is the leadership team aligned and passionate about the Vision, Mission, and Values? If not, what is your plan to align the team?

_____

_____

_____

What personnel and leadership will you need to accomplish the current, mid-term, and long-term business plan?

_____

_____

_____

Establish a budget for the wages and overhead costs of them all.

_____

_____

_____

Describe the plan for you and your leadership team to improve leadership skills and capacity, and to mature in your relationship with Christ?

_____

_____

_____

Human Resources Practices

Describe the criteria for selecting managers.

_____

_____

Describe the hiring process for employees.

_____

_____

_____

Describe the plan to review performance.

_____

_____

_____

Describe the steps leading to dismissal.

_____

_____

_____

Describe the criteria for pay raises.

_____

_____

_____

Describe any bonus system you use.

_____

_____

_____

Describe what you do for employees' retirement.

_____

_____

_____

Looking Back at Section 4:
People

React: Let's talk about it

1. What does Jesus Christ say about leading that is contrary to the way most business leaders function?

2. How would you rate yourself as a servant leader (on a scale of 1-10, with 10 being a great leader)? What can you do to improve?

3. Describe how you delegate and empower people. If you need to improve, how will you do it?

4. What does the Bible say about honesty? Have you ever been asked to take a bribe? If so, share what happened.

5. What do you do to communicate well and build trust with those with whom work?

6. Do any of your Human Resources practices need to be improved? If so, describe what you plan to do.

Help! — Online and other resources

Humility, by Andrew Murray, Baker Publishing Group

Spiritual Leadership, by J. Oswald Sanders, Moody Publishers, Chicago

Section Five: Finances

THIRTEEN

Debt

Russell Ball and James Diaz are real estate developers who made a fortune during the real estate bubble of 2003-2006. Lenders were begging them to borrow money. But when the Great Recession slammed real estate, that's when their similarities ended.

Russell had borrowed millions to renovate his residence, buy a pricey vacation home, and launch more heavily leveraged real estate projects. James learned what the Bible said about debt and paid off his home and business.

For the next five years, Russell spent most of his time squabbling with the formerly friendly lenders trying to avoid bankruptcy. James focused on buying real estate projects for pennies on the dollar. One of these men scrambled for financial survival; the other prospered.

Debt is discouraged throughout the Bible. Read the first portion of Romans 13:8 from several Bible translations: *"Owe no man anything"* (KJV). *"Let no debt remain outstanding"* (NIV). *"Pay all your debts"* (TLB). *"Owe nothing to anyone"* (NASB). *"Keep out of debt and owe no man anything"* (AMP).

In Proverbs 22:7, we learn why the Lord discourages debt: *"Just as the rich rule the poor, so the borrower is servant to the lender"* (TLB). When we are in debt, we are servants—some Bible translations use the word *slaves*—to our lenders. The more business debt we have, the more of a slave we become. We lose the freedom to decide where to spend some of the business's cash because it's already obligated to lenders.

Debt was considered a curse.

In the Old Testament, being out of debt was one of the promised rewards for obedience. *"If you diligently obey the LORD your God, being careful to do all His commandments which I command you today, the LORD your God will set you high above all the nations of the earth. All these blessings shall come upon you and overtake you if you obey the Lord your God . . . you shall lend to many nations, but you **shall not borrow**"* (Deuteronomy 28:1-2, 12, emphasis added).

On the other hand, debt was one of the curses inflicted for disobedience. *"If you do not obey the LORD your God, to observe to do all His commandments and His statutes with which I charge you today, that all these curses will come upon you . . . The alien who is among you shall rise above you higher and higher, but you will go down lower and lower.* **He shall lend to you,** *but you will not lend to him"* (Deuteronomy 28:15, 43- 44, emphasis added).

Most people think borrowing is inevitable and haven't developed a strategy for their businesses to become debt-free. And as we all have seen, the more debt businesses have, the more vulnerable they become to an unexpected economic downturn.

The decision to borrow often is based on the presumption that our business will be profitable or our job will continue in the future.

The operative word there is **presumption.**

James 4:13-14 cautions us against such a presumptive attitude: *"Come now, you who say, 'Today or tomorrow we will go to such and such a city,*

———————————————

"The borrower is slave to the lender" (Proverbs 22:7).

———————————————

and spend a year there and engage in business and make a profit.' Yet you do not know what your life will be like tomorrow."

While the Bible itself is silent about when we can borrow money for a business, I recommend this rule of thumb:

Borrow as little as possible and pay it off as quickly as possible!

Generally, there are three stages of business borrowing.

Stage 1. The owner of the business must guarantee the business debt.

When you are launching a business or it's not financially strong, lenders generally require you to personally guarantee its debt. When you personally endorse a debt, you pledge all of your assets as collateral. Many people personally guarantee business debts and don't realize that as long as the debt exists, everything they own is at risk. Proverbs 22:26-27 paints this word picture: *"Do not be among those who give pledges, among those who become guarantors for debts. If you have nothing with which to pay, why should he take your bed from under you?"*

Stage 2. The business is strong enough to borrow without the owner's guarantee.

We want to challenge you to work toward eliminating the need to personally guarantee business debts. When communicating with a lender, make certain the lender understands that the only security for the debt is the business and anything else you are pledging as collateral. You have the option of paying the debt in one of two ways: (1) in cash or, (2) with the business and the assets you have pledged as collateral. The lender has a decision to make. Do I feel good enough about the business and the collateral to loan the money? This eliminates risking all of your other assets. You are no longer slave to the lender.

Stage 3. The business is strong enough to borrow without guaranteeing the loan.

An example of this type of loan would be a well-established real estate investment company that buys an apartment complex and invests enough cash in it that a lender feels comfortable with the complex being the only security. This is the ideal way to borrow. You pledge the money you invested in an asset and the asset itself without risking the business or your other financial assets.

When mountain climbers scale a steep face of rock, they often use a technique called "tying the knots." They will climb about ten feet, hammer a spike securely in the rock, and tie their supporting rope to the spike. They do this as a safety precaution. If they slip and fall, they will fall no farther than ten feet and are usually unharmed. If, however, climbers neglect to tie the knots, a single slip can drop them a long, long ways down the cliff, resulting in serious injury or even death.

The concept of tying the knots is applicable to business and personal debt. When you pay off the debt on an asset, tie the knot! Try not to encumber the free and clear asset in case a financial slip occurs.

Dangers of Debt

In addition to the obvious financial dangers of business debt, dependence on it can also stifle creativity and mask cash flow difficulties.

Dewey Kemp and Bill Geary sensed the Lord wanted them to grow their new office supply business without using debt. This decision meant they had to think outside the box to fund expanding inventory, accounts receivable, and staff. First, they chose to sell to businesses instead of the retail market, exclusively serving companies that paid their invoices within 15 days, to minimize accounts receivable. Then they provided software that enabled customers to order product directly from their desks. A wholesale supplier delivered the products daily, radically reducing inventory and staffing needs. These and many other creative decisions enabled their company to flourish debt free.

How to Get Out of Debt

Here are four steps for getting out of debt. The goal is D-Day—Debtless Day—when your business becomes completely free of debt.

Pray.

In 2 Kings 4:1-7, a widow was threatened with losing her children to her creditor, and she appealed to the prophet Elisha for help. He told her to borrow lots of empty jars from her neighbors. Then, the Lord supernaturally multiplied her only possession—a very small amount of oil—and all the jars were filled to the brim. She sold the oil and paid her debts to free her children.

The same God who provided supernaturally for the widow is interested in your business becoming free from debt. The first and most important step is to pray. Seek the Lord's help in your journey toward Debtless Day. He can act immediately, as in the case of the widow, or slowly over time. In either case, prayer is essential.

A trend is emerging. As businesses begin to accelerate debt repayment, the Lord is blessing their faithfulness. Even if you can afford only a small monthly prepayment of your debt, do it. The Lord can multiply your efforts.

Ask good questions.

Ask these two questions about every spending category in your business:

> *Do we need this?*
>
> *If so, can we do it less expensively?*

The more profit the company generates, the quicker you can pay off the debt. Then examine every asset in your company to determine if there is anything you don't need that might be sold to help you to get out of debt more quickly.

Snowball your debt.

We've all heard people talk about "snowballing" into serious debt.

But did you know that you can snowball *out* of debt as well?

Here's how it's done. In addition to making the minimum payments on *all* your debts, focus on paying off the smallest debt first. Why the smallest balance? It's simple. Since getting out of debt can be so difficult, we all need to be encouraged by seeing the balance go down and finally to be completely paid.

After the first debt is paid off, apply its payment toward the next smallest one. After the second debt is paid off, apply what you were paying on the first and second toward the third smallest. That's the snowball in action!

This can be exciting as you see the balance really start to drop! So . . . where do you

"A trend is emerging. As businesses begin to accelerate debt repayment, the Lord is blessing their faithfulness. Even if you can afford only a small monthly prepayment of your debt, do it.

start? List your debts in order with the smallest remaining balance first. If you are disciplined and are already making progress on paying off debt, you may choose to focus on paying off the higher-interest-rate debts first even if the balances are larger.

One important step toward your company becoming debt free is to stop borrowing additional money as soon as possible. If your business depends upon credit, ask the Lord for His creativity and direction to eliminate the necessity of continued borrowing.

Don't give up!

On October 29, 1941, Winston Churchill, Prime Minister of England, gave a school commencement address. World War II was devastating Europe, and England's very fate as a nation hung in the balance. Churchill stood behind the lectern that day and said these simple words: "Never give in. Never give in. Never, never, never—in nothing, great or small, large or petty—never give in except to convictions of honor and good sense."

Allow me to encourage you with the same message.

Never, never, never give up in your effort to get out of debt. It may require hard work and sacrifice, but the freedom is worth the struggle. Remember, it's on God's heart for you and your business to become debt free.

Bankruptcy

In bankruptcy, a court of law declares a person or business unable to pay its debts. Depending upon the type of bankruptcy, the court may allow the debtor to develop a plan to repay the creditors or the court will distribute the debtor's property among the creditors as payment for the debts.

Should a godly person declare bankruptcy?

The answer is generally no.

Psalm 37:21 tells us, *"The wicked borrows and does not pay back, but the righteous is gracious and gives."* In our opinion, however, bankruptcy is permissible under two circumstances:

• If a creditor forces a person into bankruptcy, or

- If the debtor's physical or emotional health is at stake because of inability to cope with the extreme financial pressure.

After bankruptcy, seek counsel from an attorney to determine how it is legally permissible to repay the debt. Make every effort to repay it. For a large debt, this may be a long-term goal that is largely dependent on the Lord's supernatural provision of resources.

Lending

You don't have to be a banker to be in the lending business. Unless you are paid in full every time you consummate a sale, you become a lender and have to deal with credit in the form of accounts receivable. Too many businesses are damaged or fail because of lax lending or credit policies.

It is imperative that you establish a well-conceived policy for extending credit. Manage your receivables to keep bad debts at a minimum. If you have a customer who has an outstanding balance extending beyond 30 or 60 days, communicate, communicate, communicate! Remember, they very well may be using *your* credit to fund other needs in their company.

Become students of the customers who owe you money. What are vendors or others in the marketplace saying that might indicate your delinquent payers are in trouble?

If customers are unable or unwilling to pay, talk with them one on one to discuss the matter. Then listen. Although you may be frustrated or even angry, remember that your purposes in business include glorifying God and influencing people for Christ. Many businesses routinely sue those who are delinquent without making an effort to preserve the relationship.

But that's not business God's way.

We are to genuinely care for others, even if we ultimately turn the debt over to collections.

FOURTEEN

Generosity

When Chip Ingram served as pastor of his first church, he was invited to breakfast by the most successful businessman in town.

"I'd like to help the needy in town," he told Chip, "but I'm too busy. I want to deposit $5,000 in an account for you to give to those you meet who are in need. Then, let's meet once a quarter. You tell me the stories of those you helped, and I'll replenish the account."

Chip experienced amazing freedom and joy giving away the businessman's money. After about a year it dawned on him: the reason Chip enjoyed giving it so much was because it wasn't his money. That's when it dawned on him how he should view his own giving. It was never his money that he gave away, it was always the Lord's money! Recognizing that God is the owner of all you and your business possess is the key to giving generously and joyfully.

> *"Remember the words of the Lord Jesus, that He Himself said, 'It is more blessed to give than to receive'"* (Acts 20:35).

As we learned earlier, one of the purposes of being in business is to help fund the work of Christ and help those in need. Because the Lord has entrusted many Christians in business with the gift of giving, He enables them to generate income through their companies. *"We have different gifts, according to the grace given to each of us . . . if it is giving, then give generously"* (Romans 12:6, 8, NIV).

Let's examine three facets of giving that will help you and your business become generous: attitudes, advantages, and amount.

Attitudes in giving

God evaluates our giving on the basis of our attitude. *His* attitude in giving is best summed up in John 3:16: *"For God so **loved** the world, that He **gave** His only begotten Son"* (emphasis added). Did you notice the sequence? Because God loved, He gave. He set the example of giving motivated by love.

An attitude of love in giving is crucial: *"If I give all my possessions to feed the poor . . . but do not have love, it profits me nothing"* (1 Corinthians 13:3). It is hard to imagine anything more commendable than giving everything to the poor. But if it's done with the wrong attitude—without love—it doesn't benefit the giver whatsoever.

Our basis for giving out of a heart filled with love is the recognition that our gifts, though given for the benefit of people, are actually given to the Lord Himself. An example of this is Numbers 18:24: *"The tithe of the sons of Israel, which they offer as an offering to the LORD, I have given to the Levites for an inheritance."* If giving is merely to a church, a ministry, or a needy person, it's only "charity." But if it is to the Lord, it becomes an act of worship. Because God is our Creator, our Savior, and our faithful Provider, one way we can express our love is by giving our gifts to Him.

We also are to give cheerfully. *"Each one must do just as he has purposed in his heart, not grudgingly or under compulsion, for God loves a cheerful giver"* (2 Corinthians 9:7). The original Greek word for "cheerful" is "Hilarios," which translates into the English word "hilarious." We are to be hilarious givers!

Now, how do we develop this hilarity in our giving? Consider the churches of Macedonia. *"Now, brethren, we wish to make known to you the grace of God which has been given in the churches of Macedonia, that in a great ordeal of affliction and deep poverty their abundance of joy overflowed in the wealth of their liberality"* (2 Corinthians 8:1-2).

How did the Macedonians, who were in terrible circumstances—*"their great affliction and deep poverty"*—still manage to give with an *"abundance of joy"*? The answer is in verse 5: *"They first gave themselves to the Lord and to us by the will of God."* The key to cheerful giving is to submit ourselves to Christ, asking Him to direct how much He wants us to give. Only then are we in a position to give with the proper attitude and reap any of the advantages.

Stop and examine yourself. What is your attitude toward giving?

Advantages of Giving

Obviously, a gift benefits the recipient. The local church continues its ministry, the hungry are fed, and missionaries are sent. But in God's economy, the giver benefits more than the receiver. *"Remember the words of the Lord Jesus, that He Himself said, 'It is more blessed to give than to receive'"* (Acts 20:35). As we examine the Bible, we find that the giver benefits in three areas:

1. Increase in Intimacy.
Above all else, giving directs our attention and heart to Christ. Matthew 6:21 tells us, *"For where your treasure is, there will your heart be also."* Not long ago, I invested in a particular stock for the first time. Although I had never regularly checked its value before acquiring it, I found myself reading reports concerning the company and pulling up the stock on my smart phone daily. And—isn't it funny how it works?—the more money I invested in the company, the more attention I paid to it.

My heart followed my treasure.

It always works that way.

This is why it is so necessary to give each gift to the person of Jesus Christ. When you give your gift to Him, your heart will automatically be drawn to the Lord. Think of what you give as a powerful magnet that draws your heart to wherever you give–just as gravity pulls us to earth.

2. *Increase in Heaven.* Matthew 6:20 reads, *"But store up for yourselves treasures in heaven, where neither moth nor rust destroys, and where thieves do not break in or steal."* The Lord tells us that there really is something akin to the "First National Bank of Heaven." And He wants us to know that we can invest for eternity.

Paul wrote, *"Not that I seek the gift itself, but I seek for the profit which increases to your account"* (Philippians 4:17). There is a literal account for each of us in heaven that we will be privileged to enjoy for eternity. And while it is true that we "can't take it with us," the Lord reveals that we can make deposits to our heavenly account before we die.

Don't read over this too quickly.

Let this truth sink into the cracks and crevices of your mind.

YOU DON'T LOSE WHAT YOU GIVE. In fact, you will be able to enjoy it forever. It's the greatest ROI, return on investment, imaginable!

3. *Increase on Earth.* Many people believe that giving results in only spiritual blessings, not material ones, flowing to the giver. Some who hold this view are reacting to those who teach what I call "giving to get." However, Proverbs 11:24-25 reads, *"There is one who scatters, and yet increases all the more, and there is one who withholds what is justly due, and yet it results only in want. The generous man will be prosperous, and he who waters will himself be watered."*

Look at the diagram below, noticing the flow: We give, and then the Lord produces an increase, so that we may have our needs met and give even more.

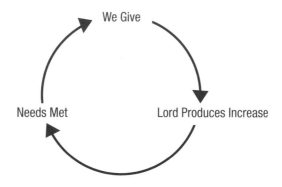

When we give from our business, we should do so with a sense of expectancy—anticipating that the Lord will provide a financial increase. What we never know is when or how the Lord may choose to provide this increase. In my experience, He can be very creative! Remember, the giver can reap the advantages of giving only when he gives cheerfully out of a heart filled with love. This precludes the motive of giving just to get.

Amount to Give

Let's survey what the Bible says about how much to give. Prior to Old Testament Law, we find two instances of giving a known amount. In Genesis 14:20, Abraham gave ten percent, a tithe, of the spoils to Melchizedek after the rescue of his nephew Lot. In Genesis 28:22, Jacob promised to give the Lord a tenth of all his possessions if God brought him safely through his journey.

The Old Testament Law required a tithe. The Lord condemns the children of Israel in Malachi 3:8-9 for not tithing properly: *"Will a man rob God? Yet you are robbing Me! But you say, 'How have we robbed You?' In tithes and offerings. You are cursed with a curse, for you are robbing Me, the whole nation of you!"* In addition to the tithe, the Law specified various offerings.

> *Should businesses give from net or gross income? As a rule of thumb, give based on the net income after expenses.*

In the New Testament, the tithe is neither specifically required nor rejected. The instruction is to give in proportion to the material blessing we have received—with special commendation for sacrificial giving.

What we like about the tithe is that it's systematic, and the amount of the gift is easy to compute. A danger of the tithe is the view that once I've given my ten percent, I have fulfilled all my obligations to give. For many godly businesspeople, the tithe should be the beginning of their giving, not the limit of their giving.

Businesspeople often ask if their businesses should give from net or gross income. As a rule of thumb, I recommend giving based on the net income after expenses, because many businesses operate on a small profit margin.

So how much should you and your business give? Don't answer this question by immediately getting out your calculator or double-checking your books. Answer this question by first giving yourself afresh to the Lord. Submit yourself to Him. Earnestly seek His will for you in this area, asking Him to help you obey Christ's leading. A very generous businesswoman expressed it this way: "The profitability of your business determines the potential of how much you *can* give. Your vision for your business determines how much you *will* give."

Places to Give

The Bible instructs us to give to the local church, ministries, and the poor and needy. Let's focus on what the Lord says about caring for the needy, because there are hundreds of verses that address it. Matthew 25:34-45 teaches one of the most exciting and yet sobering truths in the Bible. Read this passage carefully.

> "The King will say, 'For I was hungry and you gave Me something to eat; I was thirsty, and you gave Me something to drink.' Then . . . the righteous will answer Him, 'Lord, when did we see You hungry, and feed You, or thirsty, and give You something to drink?' . . . The King will answer and say to them . . . 'To the extent that you did it to one of these brothers of Mine, even the least of them, **you did it to Me.**'
>
> "Then He will also say to those on His left, 'Depart from Me, accursed ones, into the eternal fire . . . for I was hungry, and you gave Me nothing to eat; I was thirsty, and you gave Me nothing to drink . . . To the extent that you did not do it to one of the least of these, you **did not do it to Me** (emphasis added).'"

In a mysterious way we can't fully understand, Jesus, the Creator of all things, personally identifies Himself with the poor. When we share with the needy, we are actually sharing with Jesus Himself. If that truth is staggering, then this is terrifying: when we refuse or neglect to give to the needy, we leave Christ Himself hungry and thirsty.

Three areas of our life are affected by whether we give to the poor.

> **Prayer.** A lack of giving to the poor could be a source of unanswered prayer. *"Is this not the fast which I choose . . . to divide your bread with the hungry and bring the homeless poor into the house?. . . Then you will call and the LORD will answer"* (Isaiah 58:6-9).

> **Provision.** Our giving to the needy may determine our provision. *"He who gives to the poor will never want, but he who shuts his eyes will have many curses"* (Proverbs 28:27).

> **Knowing Jesus Christ intimately.** Those who refuse or neglect to share resources with the poor don't know the Lord as intimately as they could. *" 'He pled the cause of the afflicted and the needy; then it was well. Is that not what it means to know Me?' declares the LORD"* (Jeremiah 22:16).

If you don't already know some needy people, please consider asking the Lord to bring one into your life. You can do so by praying this prayer: "Father God, create in me the desire to share with the needy. Bring a poor person into my life so that I might learn what it means to give."

May we in the business community echo Job's statement: *"I delivered the poor who cried for help, and the orphan who had no helper . . . I made the widow's heart sing for joy . . . I was eyes to the blind and feet to the lame. I was a father to the needy, and **I investigated the case which I did not know**"* (Job 29:12-16, emphasis added).

Creative Giving

Some Christians in business also donate some of their products or services. Compass, for example, receives donated airtime from hundreds of radio stations to broadcast the programs *MoneyWise* and *HeyHoward*. A couple provide Compass free space in their office building. Others have donated real estate or company stock, which can be a tax-advantaged way to give.

Creating a Culture of Generosity

The First Southern story began in 1982 when Jess Correll acquired a small bank in Stanford, Kentucky, a rural community. The bank grew using a great deal of leverage. In the early 90s, CEO, Jess Correll, and his leadership team enrolled in what is now the Compass *Navigating Your Finances God's Way* small group study. The study completely changed how they operate the company.

First, they began to give ten percent of their corporate earnings, later establishing a foundation to administer this generosity.

The study also convinced them of the wisdom of using debt sparingly. With earnings, they retired most of their debt by 1994. They resolved to remain a low-debt company, limiting acquisitions to short-term debt that they projected they could pay off in three years or less.

Jess Correll and his team have been on a self-described journey of generosity and weaning themselves off of debt. Their mantra is: Debt is Bad, Saving is Good, Giving is Joyful, and Stuff is Meaningless.

Their philosophy of generosity is "Live to Give." This corporate value is practiced by the entire First Southern family. Every employee is eligible to receive an annual matching gift up to $1,000 for giving to a charitable cause. In addition, they encourage their staff to go on mission trips to serve those in need around the world. First Southern pays 75 percent of the cost of the first trip and 50 percent of a second.

In 2008, when the Great Recession crisis slammed the banking system, First Southern's profit plummeted more than 30 percent. They were faced with a challenging decision. Even though they were current on all their debt payments, should they reduce their giving to focus on paying off all their debt so the bank would be more stable financially?

Because the board of directors was fully committed to giving ten percent of earning, First Southern never wavered in its generosity.

Interestingly, since First Southern had only a small amount of debt, they were able to be opportunistic and to purchase deeply discounted mortgages during the crisis. They became financially stronger through it. They also made the decision to pay off all debt and grow only as the Lord provides the resources.

FIFTEEN

Business Structure

The legal structure you choose for your business will have a lot to do with its success or failure. The most common forms of business are the sole proprietorship, partnership, corporation and limited liability company (LLC). People enter into a partnership or form a corporation or LLC to raise capital, to bring expertise or labor to a business, for tax considerations, and to create a shield from liability.

Let's examine some of the most common business structures.

Partnerships

The Bible clearly discourages business partnerships with those who don't know Christ. "*Do not be bound together* [unequally yoked] *with unbelievers; for what partnership have righteousness and lawlessness, or what fellowship has light with darkness? Or what . . . has a believer in common with an unbeliever? . . . 'Therefore, come out from their midst and be separate, says the Lord'*" (2 Corinthians 6:14-17).

There are some practices in the Bible that seem to be fall into "gray areas," neither good nor bad.

This isn't one of them.

Why does Scripture wave such an obvious red flag in the matter of joining forces with non-Christians in a business partnership? Because God knows it would result in an inevitable train wreck of conflicting values.

Jose, a committed follower of Christ, entered into a partnership with a brilliant engineer to manufacture high-tech machinery. Even though the engineer didn't personally know Christ, their skills complemented each other, and the company initially flourished.

Later, however, Jose was pressured by his partner to compromise his integrity to market one of their products. When he refused, their relationship was strained. It became obvious to Jose that his love for Christ and his desire to operate the business God's way annoyed his partner. Finally, Jose decided he had to exit the partnership.

In our opinion, we should also be extremely careful before entering into ANY business partnership, even one with another person who knows Christ. The fact of the matter is, far too many Christian partnerships end badly. With my lifetime of contacts, I would consider only a few people as partners. These are people I have known well for years. I've observed their commitment to the Lord, know their strengths and weaknesses, and have seen them handle money faithfully in difficult situations.

> *Before forming a partnership, carefully document in writing what you agree upon. Partners often have different expectations and may remember their understandings differently. Someone once said the palest ink is better than the best memory.*

Before forming a partnership, carefully document in writing what you agree upon. Partners often have different expectations and may remember their understandings differently. Someone once said the palest ink is better than the best memory. Develop your agreement in detail. If you are not able to agree in writing, don't tie the business knot with that individual. Don't become partners.

Here are some issues you should address together:

- Develop the business plan.
- Identify the vision, mission, and values of the business.
- Who will be in charge?
- How much capital will be invested initially, and who will invest it? What will we do if more capital is necessary?
- What happens if a partner wants to leave the partnership or terminate it?
- What is the job description of each partner and how many hours a week will each work?
- What happens if a partner consistently works fewer hours than agreed upon?

One final observation: a partnership usually won't survive if an equal partner contributes significantly more to its success than the other.

Limited Liability Business

When a corporation, a LLC, or a limited liability partnership (LLP) is owned by two people holding equal shares, treat this business relationship as if it were a partnership. Don't be bound to those who don't know Christ, and execute an agreement in writing.

Forming a corporation, LLC, or LLP will help limit the liability of losses or a lawsuit to the business, and act as a shield to help protect the owners. An added benefit of a LLC or LLP is that for tax purposes it is treated as a normal partnership.

Litigation

In our day, lawsuits are as common as dandelions in an untended lawn. Thousands are filed each day. Tragically, many of these suits pit Christian against Christian. The court system uses an adversarial judicial process that frequently creates animosities and fractures relationships between parties. Instead of trying to heal wounds, the system provides a legal solution—but leaves the problems of unforgiveness and anger untouched and unresolved.

The Bible, however, holds forth reconciliation as the goal.

"Therefore if you are presenting your offering at the altar, and there remember that your brother has something against you, leave your offering there before the altar and go; first be reconciled to your brother" (Matthew 5:23-24).

Scripture clearly states that when Christians are at odds with each other, they should try not to settle their disputes through the courts. *"Does any one of you, when he has a case against his neighbor, dare to go to law before the unrighteous and not before the saints?. . .but brother goes to law with brother, and that before unbelievers? Actually, then, it is already a defeat for you, that you have lawsuits with one another. Why not rather be wronged? Why not rather be defrauded?"* (1 Corinthians 6:1-7).

Instead of initiating a lawsuit, Jesus sets forth a three-step procedure for settling differences in Matthew 18:15-17: *"If your brother sins, go and show him his fault in private; if he listens to you, you have won your brother. But if he does not listen to you, take one or two more with you, so that by the mouth of two or three witnesses every fact may be confirmed. If he refuses to listen to them, tell it to the church; and if he refuses to listen even to the church, let him be to you as a Gentile and a tax collector."*

Based on this passage, you should handle a dispute with another Christian this way:

1. **Go in private.** Meet one on one and try to agree upon a resolution of your differences.

2. **Go with one or two others.** If the one-on-one meeting fails, seek to meet again and add others who know the facts.

3. **Go before the church.** If the other party isn't willing to find a reasonable solution, ask if they would join you in submitting to Christian arbitration. If they are still unwilling to try to resolve the matter, you have the option of the courts. Before initiating such a lawsuit, however, pray and reflect on Luke 6:30, *"Give to everyone who asks*

of you, and whoever takes away what is yours, do not demand it back."

The greatest benefit of following this procedure isn't simply reaching a fair settlement, but practicing forgiveness and demonstrating love.

Taxes

What does the Bible say about paying taxes? That's the same question that was asked of Jesus. *"Is it lawful for us to pay taxes to Caesar, or not?. . .* [Jesus] *said to them, 'Show Me a* [Roman coin]. *Whose likeness and inscription does it have?' They said, 'Caesar's.' And He said to them, 'Then give to Caesar the things that are Caesar's . . .'"* (Luke 20:22-25).

The Bible clearly tells us to pay our taxes. *"Every person is to be in subjection to the governing authorities. For there is no authority except from God, and those which exist are established by God . . . because of this you also pay taxes, for rulers are servants of God, devoting themselves to this very thing. Render to all what is due them: tax to whom tax is due"* (Romans 13:1, 6-7). It's certainly permissible to reduce business or personal taxes by using legal tax deductions, but we should be careful not to make unwise decisions simply to avoid paying taxes.

It's time for a personal confession here.

For years I had a terrible attitude about paying taxes. Just thinking about it robbed me of my joy. But then I considered what it must have been like for Jesus and the people of Israel living under brutal Roman rule. And even in that harsh setting, Jesus instructed His people to pay taxes to the governing authorities. I am grateful to the Lord for allowing me to live in my country. This has changed my attitude to one of thankfulness when I pay taxes.

Startups and Entrepreneurs

Startups often require months or even years of effort before they become profitable or produce enough income to pay a salary to the entrepreneur-founder. Therefore, you need to get your personal finances as healthy as possible by paying off debt and increasing your savings *before* launching a new business. Far too many people begin a business on a shoestring when they already are having difficulty making ends meet.

When you start a business, it's critical for you to stay on top of the company's finances. Be sure you maintain a business checking account separate from your personal account. This will enable you to track income and expenses quickly and determine whether the business is profitable. Then produce a monthly Profit & Loss Statement using one of the simple, effective accounting systems available today. And don't forget to set aside money to pay taxes and fund employee benefits.

Many husband and wife teams have succeeded in launching businesses because one focused on sales and the other on bookkeeping.

Business Plan

BALANCE SHEET

The Balance Sheet is intended to provide a snapshot of the financial health of your business by focusing on its assets and liabilities. Someone once said, "Just let the numbers speak to you. We tend to believe the business is doing better or worse than it really is, but the numbers are an accurate barometer. So, just let the numbers speak to you."

Most business people concentrate on reviewing the monthly Profit & Loss Statement, but it is equally important to study the Balance Sheet. You need to follow the trends of your cash, accounts receivable, inventory, payables, and other indicators.

Balance Sheet

ASSETS		LIABILITIES	
Cash	_____	Notes Payable	_____
Accounts Rec	_____	Accounts Payable	_____
Inventory	_____	Wages Payable	_____
Supplies	_____	Interest Payable	_____
Prepaid Ins	_____	Taxes Payable	_____
Investments	_____	Mortgages Payable	_____
Land	_____	Notes Payable	_____
Buildings	_____	Total Liabilities	_____
Equipment	_____		
Vehicles	_____	**STOCKHOLDERS' EQUITY**	
Less Accum	_____	Common Stock	_____
Depreciation		Retained Earnings	_____
Other Assets	_____	*Less Treasury Stock*	_____
Total Assets	_____	*Stockholder Equity*	_____
		Total Liabilities &	_____
		Stock Holders Equity	

Profit and Loss Statement

The Profit & Loss Statement is intended to provide a snapshot of your business's income, spending, and net profit or loss. Review it monthly to identify the trends of your income, expenses, surplus or deficit, and other critical indicators. The Profit & Loss Statement below will most likely need to be customized for your business.

INCOME

Sales Revenue   _____

Interest Income   _____

Investment Income   _____

Other Income   _____   TOTAL INCOME _____

EXPENSES

Accounting Services   _____

Advertising   _____

Bank Service Charges   _____

Cost of Goods   _____

Estimated Taxes   _____

Health Insurance   _____

Interest   _____

Legal Expenses   _____

Office Supplies   _____

Payroll & Payroll Taxes _____

Printing   _____

Professional Fees   _____

Rent/Lease Payments   _____

Retirement Contribs   _____

Utilities and Telephone _____

Other Expenses   _____   TOTAL EXPENSES _____

                                   SURPLUS/(DEFICIT)_____

Looking Back at Section 5: Finances

React: Let's talk about it

1. Is debt encouraged in Scripture? Why? If you are in debt, what is your strategy to get out of it?

2. Share the most difficult time you have had, either in business or in your personal finances, because of debt.

3. What did you learn about giving that was helpful or challenging?

4. Describe how you are giving from business, or how you want it to become more generous.

5. Carefully review your Balance Sheet and Profit & Loss Statement. What are their strengths and weaknesses? What will you do to improve the weaknesses and capitalize on the strengths?

6. What are the three most important things you need to do increase the profitability of your business?

Help! -- Online and other resources

Free and Clear, by Howard Dayton, Moody Publishers, Chicago

The Treasure Principle, by Randy Alcorn, Multnomah Publishers, Sisters, Oregon

Generous Giving, generousgiving.org, has many proven resources to help you become more generous

National Christian Foundation, nationalchristian.com is a respected donor advised fund.

Brian Kluth, GiveWithJoy.org, is an outstanding generosity author and speaker

Section Six: Finishing Well

SIXTEEN

Crisis

S tarting from scratch, the three Schrimsher brothers built a highly respected real estate investment company in Central Florida. For three decades, Steve, Frank, and Michael operated their business based squarely on the principles of the Bible—hard work, integrity, and no personal or business debt—and the business thrived.

On June 25, 2008, everything changed.

Without warning, their largest partner committed suicide. Shockingly, over the weeks that followed, they discovered that he had embezzled and spent about $33 million dollars from their partnerships!

It was front page news, and the Schrimshers were scrambling for survival. Their reputation was in tatters, and they were threatened with lawsuits from panicked investors. They needed to finish half-completed apartment projects owned by the defrauded partnerships. They over-communicated with their investors and were fully transparent even when the news was bad.

During one particularly discouraging time, Steve's wife told him, "We started with nothing, and if we lose everything, we still have each other.

More importantly, we still have Christ."

Frank added, "All we could do was to wake up every morning and say to ourselves, 'Today we're going to do the right thing, no matter what.' And we prayed that the Lord would honor our faithfulness and hard work.'" And the Lord has been gracious to do just that.

Unexpectedly, two large insurance policies covering their partner's life were assigned to them to pay back about 40 percent of the money stolen. Several projects were completed and sold to recover more of the money.

Steve said, "We thought our partner was as committed to Jesus Christ and His way of doing business, just as we were. He joined us on mission trips, and he was very generous to his church and several ministries. He knew all the right words to give us confidence in his relationship with Christ."

To date, about three-fourths of the money has been returned to the investors. The Schrimshers remain committed to do all they can to return every penny that was lost. Amazingly, their reputation is better today than it was before they learned of the embezzlement!

A friend once told me—and only half in jest—"Everyone goes through crises. You've either just come out of one, or you're in the middle of one, or you're just about to go into one—you just don't know it yet."

If we have an inadequate or warped view of God and His purposes, then we won't fully embrace and learn from our challenges. What's more, we will forfeit the peace, contentment, and even joy that God makes available to us in the midst of the storm.

Some challenges build slowly and can be anticipated; others strike like a bolt out of the blue. Some are resolved quickly; others are chronic. Some reflect the consequences of our actions; others are completely beyond our control. Some crises impact an entire nation; others are isolated to our business or to us as individuals.

The loss of a key employee, a change in technology or your market, new competition, a worldwide financial crisis, or a host of other challenges can exert major pressure on us and our business.

I call these challenges the "storms of life." While some of the storms amount to little more than a blustery rain shower, others feel like a category-five hurricane.

Please remember this one thing: No matter what the crisis, you don't face it alone. Put yourself in the sandals of a few of God's people in the Bible who faced terrifying category-five storms.

- Job—in a matter of just a few hours—lost his children, his financial resources, and finally his health.
- Joseph was sold into slavery, then falsely accused and thrown into prison.
- Moses and the children of Israel faced annihilation by Egypt's powerful army in a cul-de-sac at the Red Sea.
- Daniel was tossed into the lion's den.
- Paul was beaten, stoned and left for dead, chained, and imprisoned on his missionary journeys.

The list goes on and on.

Although storms are often emotional, scary, and painful, if we maintain God's perspective, we can survive and even grow through such dark days (and nights!).

God's Role

When facing a crisis, *nothing* is more important than knowing **who God is**—His love, care, control, and power. Only the Bible reveals the true extent of God's involvement in our challenges. If we have an inadequate or warped view of God and His purposes, then we won't fully embrace and learn from our challenges. What's more, we will forfeit the peace, contentment, and even joy that God makes available to us in the midst of the storm.

God Loves You.

First John 4:8 sums up God's very nature: *"God is love."* God loves you, and throughout your whole life remains intimately involved with you as an individual. Psalm 139:17 reveals, *"How precious it is, Lord, to realize that you are thinking about me constantly! I can't even count how many times a day your thoughts turn towards me"* (TLB).

John 15:9 has to be one of the most encouraging verses in all of the Bible. Jesus says: *"As the Father has loved me, so I have loved you"* (NIV). Don't skim over those words! Let the implications sink in for a moment. Consider how much God the Father loves God the Son. They have existed forever in the closest possible relationship with a deep, unfathomable love for each other.

And Jesus says this is how much He loves you?

Could it be? Yes it is.

In any crisis it's critical to be reminded of God's unfailing love and faithfulness. Why? Because it's so very easy to become discouraged and even lose hope. It's easy to forget God's love and care for you, especially when adversity first strikes—or goes on and on for what feels like an eternity.

Jeremiah the prophet was completely discouraged. He wrote: *"I remember my affliction and my wandering, the bitterness . . . my soul is downcast within me"* (Lamentations 3:19-20, NIV). But then he remembered the Lord, *"Yet I call this to mind and therefore have hope. Because of the LORD's great love we are not consumed, for his compassions never fail. They are new every morning; great is your faithfulness"* (Lamentations 3:21-23, NIV).

"Consider it pure joy, my brothers and sisters, whenever you face trials of many kinds, because you know that the testing of your faith develops perseverance. Let perseverance finish its work so that you may be mature and complete, not lacking anything" (James 1:2-4).

It is helpful to meditate on passages such as these: *"God has said, 'Never will I leave you; never will I forsake you.' So we can say with confidence, 'The Lord is my helper; I will not be afraid. What can mere mortals do to me?'"* (Hebrews 13:5-6, NIV). *"Who shall separate us from the love of Christ? Shall trouble or hardship or persecution or famine or nakedness or danger or sword? . . . No, in all these things we are more than conquerors through him who loved us"* (Romans 8:35, 37, NIV).

Even in a crisis, the Lord will do kind things that offer unmistakable evidence of His care for us—if we are willing to open our eyes and see them. Consider Joseph. While he was a slave, *"[Joseph's] master saw that the Lord was with him"* (Genesis 39:3), so his master put him in charge of all he owned. Later in prison, *"the Lord was with Joseph and extended kindness to him, and gave him favor in the sight of the chief jailer"* (Genesis 39:21).

God Is In Control.

God is ultimately in control of every event. This is but a sampling of passages that affirm His control: *"Our God is in the heavens; He does whatever He pleases"* (Psalm 115:3). *"We adore you as being in control of everything"* (1 Chronicles 29:11, TLB). *"Whatever the Lord pleases, He does, in heaven and in earth"* (Psalm 135:6). *"For nothing will be impossible with God"* (Luke 1:37).

The Lord is in control even of seemingly dark, difficult events. *"I am the LORD, and there is no other, the One forming light and creating darkness, causing well-being and creating calamity; I am the LORD who does all these"* (Isaiah 45:6-7).

God Has a Purpose for Adversity

The Cecropia moth emerges from its cocoon only after a long, exhausting struggle to free itself. A young boy, wishing to help the moth, carefully slit the exterior of the cocoon. Soon it came out, but its wings were shriveled, and couldn't function. What the young boy didn't realize was that the moth's struggle to liberate itself from the cocoon was essential to develop its wings—and its ability to fly.

Much like the cocoon of the moth, adversity has a part to play in our lives as well. God uses those difficult, sometimes heartbreaking times to mature us in Christ. The Apostle James says it this way: *"Consider it **pure joy**, my brothers and sisters, whenever you face trials of many kinds, because you know that the testing of your faith develops perseverance. Let perseverance finish its work so that you may be mature and complete, not lacking anything"* (James 1:2-4, NIV, emphasis added).

Pure joy?

Facing trials of many kinds?

Was James in his right mind when he wrote those words?

Yes, he was. The apostle told us how to regard all of the difficulty that crashes into our lives. We're to consider it joy. Why? Because it can lead to a closer relationship with Jesus Christ.

God designs challenging circumstances for our ultimate benefit. Romans 8:28-29 tells us, *"We know that in all things God works for the good of those who love him, who have been called according to his purpose. For those God foreknew he also predestined to be conformed to the image of his Son"* (NIV). And the primary good that God works in our lives is to make us more like Christ.

We see this same thought expressed in Hebrews 12:6, 10-11, *"For those whom the Lord loves He disciplines . . . He disciplines us for our good, so that we may share His holiness. All discipline for the moment seems not to be joyful, but sorrowful; yet to those who have been trained by it, afterwards it yields the peaceful fruit of righteousness."* No matter what our roller-coaster emotions might tell us at times, God makes no mistakes. He knows exactly what He wants us to become, and He also knows exactly what is necessary to produce that result in our lives.

Alan Redpath captures this truth:

> There is nothing—no circumstances, no trouble, no testing—that can ever touch me until, first of all, it has gone past God, past Christ, right through to me. If it has come that far, it has come with great purpose, which I may not understand at the moment. But as I refuse to panic, as I lift my eyes to Him and accept it as coming from the throne of God for some great purpose of blessing to my own heart, no sorrow will ever disturb me, no trial will ever disarm me, no circumstance will cause me to fret, for I shall rest in the joy of who my Lord is.

Bev and I have endured —and benefited from—many storms. From the birth and death of a precious special-needs child, to an unwanted career change, to Bev's double mastectomy and the breast cancer spreading to her bones. Through the crucible of our pain and tears, many of the Bible's truths grew from wispy theory into rock-solid reality. Although we would never want to repeat these experiences, we are incredibly grateful for how the Lord used them in our lives.

Author Ron Dunn observed: "If God subtracted one pain, one heartache, one disappointment from my life, I would be less than the person I am now, less the person God wants me to be, and my ministry would be less than He intends."

Please don't miss this point. You and I need to recognize difficulties as opportunities to grow into the people God wants us to be. In adversity we learn things we just couldn't learn any other way.

I know what you're thinking . . . "Easy for you to say, Howard. You have no idea what we've been through." Granted. But then, I could also say, "You have no idea what *we* have been through during our business career and 42 years of marriage." And yet the Lord Jesus has stood with us in every crisis, every heartache, every difficult decision. Every one of those incidents, painful as they were, brought us closer to Him and closer to each other.

> *The key to solving your business and financial problems is learning and practicing God's way of handling money and operating a business. Yes, it truly is that simple.*

You can be comforted knowing that your loving heavenly Father is in absolute control of every situation you will ever face. He intends to use each circumstance for a good purpose. First Thessalonians 5:18 says it well, *"Give thanks in **all** circumstances, for this is God's will for you in Christ Jesus (emphasis added)."*

Trusting God

We should view crises through the lens of God's love, faithfulness, and control. The Bible makes it clear that God offers security only in Himself—not in business, not in money, not in a career, and not in other people. External things offer the illusion of security, but the Lord alone can be fully trusted. *"The LORD is good, a refuge in times of trouble. He cares for those who trust in him"* (Nahum 1:7, NIV). *"When I am afraid, I will put my trust in you. In God, whose word I praise, in God I have put my trust; I shall not be afraid"* (Psalm 56:3-4).

The Eye of the Storm

There are several things we can do to survive—and even grow—when we find ourselves in a storm.

Get your finances in order.

I've been close to many people facing gut-wrenching financial storms. And the first question they usually ask is, how can I solve the problem? Jesus answers the question this way in Matthew 7:24-25: *"Everyone who hears these words of mine and **puts them into practice** is like a wise man who built his house on the rock. The rain came down, the streams rose, and the winds blew and beat against that house; yet it did not fall, because it had its foundation on the rock"* (NIV, emphasis added).

The key to solving your business and financial problems is learning and practicing God's way of handling money and operating a business.

Yes, it truly is that simple.

That's why this book is so important. When you finish it, you will know God's framework for managing a business. But *knowing* is only half of what you need. The other half is *applying* what you have learned. It may take a long time and a lot of effort to navigate the storm, but you will know the basics of what you should do.

James 1:22-25 bluntly emphasizes the importance of application: *"Do not merely listen to the word, and so deceive yourselves. Do what it says. . . . whoever looks intently into the perfect law that gives freedom, and continues in it, not forgetting what they have heard, but doing it—they will be blessed in what they do"* (NIV). Don't compromise or be half-hearted in implementing what the Lord has revealed about operating a business. As the James passage instructs us—do what it says so that you will be blessed in what you do.

Part of what you've already learned is to be a generous giver. When facing a financial crisis, the tendency is to hold on tightly to what we have and to become less generous. A passage in the book of Acts, however, shows us a different way. In Acts 11:28-29 we read: *"Agabus [a prophet] . . . through the Spirit predicted that a severe famine would spread over the entire Roman world. (This happened during the reign of*

Claudius.) The disciples, as each one was able, decided to provide help for the brothers and sisters living in Judea" (NIV).

Consider this. The Holy Spirit revealed that a severe famine was coming soon, and their first reaction was to get out their checkbooks! Don't allow a crisis to stop you from remaining generous. You may not be able to give as much as you did previously, but still give.

It's also important to quickly evaluate how the circumstance will impact your business and finances, and to make adjustments for any diminished income or increased expenses. And if you are married, tell your spouse your feelings and concerns.

How important is this?

It's important enough to schedule a time *every day* to pray and share, so you can encourage each other. Bev and I discovered that a crisis doesn't have to damage our marriage; in fact, it can be a catalyst to improve it. I am fully persuaded that God intends married couples to grow closer together during a crisis rather than allowing the difficulties to damage their marriage.

Never go through a storm alone.

Without repeating the advice of seeking counsel, I want to emphasize the importance of not going it alone. It's almost impossible to make the wisest decisions in isolation when experiencing a crisis.

Seek advice from people who have been through similar situations. You will draw strength not only from their emotional support but also from their experience. There are people all around you who have weathered similar storms, and you can gain from their knowledge, learning mistakes to avoid and resources to help. Ask your church and friends to pray; it's their most powerful contribution.

Live one day at a time.

Robert Johnson built an extraordinarily successful construction business from scratch. He was extremely generous and enjoyed a wonderful reputation. And then came the crushing financial crisis of 2008—crippling his business and pushing him to the brink of bankruptcy.

Confiding in me one day, Robert said, "In a crisis, the tendency is to look ahead and become overwhelmed with all the problems. We are to plan ahead, but for our mental and emotional health we must follow what Jesus Christ told us: *". . . do not worry about tomorrow, for tomorrow will worry about itself. Each day has enough trouble of its own"* (Matthew 6:34, NIV).

Live focused on today! And if the crisis becomes super severe, focus on one moment at a time in close fellowship with Christ.

Is this an escape from reality?

No, it is embracing Ultimate Reality.

It is a practical method to stay close to the only one who can help through the challenge.

Be patient, waiting for God's timing.

Expectations can be damaging during a crisis. When we assume that the Lord will solve our problems in a certain way by a certain time, we set ourselves up for disappointment and frustration.

Someone described patience as accepting a difficult situation without giving God a deadline for removing it. Remember, God's primary purpose in allowing a crisis in the first place is to conform you to Jesus Christ. He is at work in your life, and He knows exactly how long it will take to produce the results He wants.

The late Larry Burkett used to say with a smile, "God is seldom early, but He's never late." Be patient. Be careful not to set deadlines for the Lord to act.

Work diligently to solve your own problems, with the recognition that you need the moment by moment help and counsel of the Lord who loves you. Philippians 4:6-7 is one of my favorite passages when facing difficulties. Every phrase is loaded with meaning. *"Be anxious for nothing, but in everything by prayer and supplication with thanksgiving let your request be made known to God. And the peace of God, which surpasses all comprehension, will guard your hearts and your minds in Christ Jesus."*

On the morning of September 29, 1982, twelve-year-old Mary Kellerman died after taking a capsule of Extra-Strength Tylenol. Soon after, six other people died, all from the Chicago area. It was discovered that bottles of Tylenol had been tampered with and laced with cyanide. Within 24 hours of the public learning of this tragedy, Tylenol's market share collapsed from 35 percent to 5 percent, and the reputation of its manufacturer, Johnson & Johnson, was seriously threatened.

Johnson & Johnson's CEO, Dr. James E. Burke, a Christian, acted decisively. He assembled a seven-member team of his top managers to focus on the crisis. Johnson & Johnson's CFO warned Dr. Burke that a total recall of Tylenol would cost the company more than $150 million.

Dr. Burke quickly issued a nationwide recall of Tylenol products; an estimated 31 million bottles were in circulation. The company advertised in the media for consumers not to consume any Tylenol products. They also stopped manufacturing and advertising Tylenol.

Johnson & Johnson set up a toll-free 800 number for customers to call if they had questions. Dr. Burke installed a live satellite feed into his office so he could stay on top of the situation and regularly made himself available to the media. He communicated truthfully and announced that Tylenol was going to innovate and use safety seal packing—something none of his competitors were using.

When the accountants warned Dr. Burke that these decisions were going to cost more than $150 million, Dr. Burke responded, "Do you remember our company's Credo? Our first responsibility is to our customers. It's worth spending $150 million if it saves lives."

Afterwards, the media gave Johnson & Johnson credit for handling the crisis extraordinarily well. *The Washington Post* wrote, "Johnson & Johnson has effectively demonstrated how a major business ought to handle a disaster." They were applauded for their honesty and the care they exhibited for people.

Customers responded as well. Within a year, their market share had rebounded and actually increased. Dr. Burke later recalled, "Whenever we cared for the customer in a profound and spiritual way, profits were never a problem."

SEVENTEEN

Eternity

On Monday, October 25, 1999, the news reported an unfolding story. Air Force jets following a Learjet from Orlando, Florida, were unable to communicate with its pilots. I learned later that two very close friends and accomplished businessmen, Robert Fraley and Van Ardan, were on that Learjet as it carried them and golfer Payne Stewart to their deaths.

One of the most critical principles for us to understand when operating a business and handling money is the reality of eternity. Robert and Van, in their mid-forties, lived with an eternal perspective. Robert had framed these words of Saint Augustine in his workout area: "Take care of your body as though you will live forever; take care of your soul as though you will die tomorrow."

Because God loves us, He reveals in the Bible that there is a heaven and hell, that there is a coming judgment, and that He will grant eternal rewards. The Lord wants the very best for us. For this reason, He wants to motivate us to invest our lives, businesses, and finances in such a way that we can enjoy an intimate relationship with Him now—and receive the greatest possible rewards in the life to come.

Our failure to view our present lives through the lens of eternity is one of the biggest hindrances to seeing our lives and our businesses in their true light. Yet Scripture states that the reality of our eternal future should determine the character of our present lives, how we operate our businesses and use our money.

People who don't know the Lord look at life as a brief interval that begins at birth and ends at death. Looking to the future, they see no further than their own life span. Beyond their years on earth there is . . . nothing. A zero. A blank. With no eternal perspective, they think, *If this life is all there is, why deny myself anything?*

Those who know Christ have an entirely different perspective. We know life is short. It's the preface, not the book. It's the preliminary, not the main event. Yet this brief testing period will determine much of our experience in heaven.

Business consultants and financial planners try to persuade people to look down the road instead of simply focusing on today. "Don't think in terms of this year," they will tell you. "Think and plan for

"Show me, Lord, my life's end and the number of my days; let me know how fleeting my life is. . . . Everyone is but a breath . . . a mere phantom . . . heaping up wealth without knowing whose it will finally be"
(Psalm 39:4-6, NIV).

30 years from now." The wise person does indeed think ahead, but far more than 30 years ahead—more like 30 *million* years ahead. Someone once said, "He who provides for this life but takes no care for eternity is wise for a moment but a fool forever." Jesus said it this way: *"What does it profit a man to gain the whole world, and forfeit his soul?"* (Mark 8:36).

The Long and Short of It

The Bible frequently reminds us that life on earth is brief: *"[God] is mindful that we are but dust"* (Psalm 103:14). David recognized this and sought to gain God's perspective on the brevity of life. He asked of the Lord, *"Show me, Lord, my life's end and the number of my days; let me know how fleeting my life is. . . . Everyone is but a breath . . . a mere phantom . . . heaping up wealth without knowing whose it will finally be"* (Psalm 39:4-6, NIV).

Moses realized that true wisdom flowed out of understanding that our lives are short. With that in mind, he asked the Lord to help him number the days he had on earth. *"As for the days of our life, they contain seventy years, or if due to strength, eighty years . . . for soon it is gone and we fly away. . . . So teach us to number our days, that we may present to You a heart of wisdom"* (Psalm 90:10, 12).

I encourage you to estimate the number the days that you have left on earth. If I live as long as my father (which is no sure thing), I have about 5,500 days left. This has helped me become aware that I need to invest my life and resources in efforts that will count for eternity.

Eternity Is Long

If life on earth is brief, ending all too quickly, eternity *never ends.* It is forever. Imagine a cable running through the room where you are now. To your right, the cable runs billions of light years, all the way to the end of the universe; to your left, it runs to the other end of the universe. Now imagine that the cable to your left represents eternity past, and the cable to your right, eternity future. Take out a pencil and make a small mark on the cable in front of you. That tiny mark represents your brief life on earth.

Eternity Past   Eternity Future

Because most people don't have an eternal perspective, they live as if the mark were all there is. They make *mark* choices, manage *mark* businesses, live in *mark* houses, drive *mark* cars, wear *mark* clothes, and raise *mark* children. Devotional writer A. W. Tozer referred to eternity as "the long tomorrow." This is the backdrop against which all the questions of life and our business career must be answered.

Aliens and Pilgrims

Scripture tells us several things about our identity and role on earth. First, *"Our citizenship is in heaven"* (Philippians 3:20), not on earth. Second, *"We are ambassadors for Christ"* (2 Corinthians 5:20), representing Him on earth. Imagine yourself as an ambassador working in a country that is generally hostile toward your own. Naturally, you want to learn about this new place, see the sights, and become familiar with the people and culture. But suppose you eventually become so assimilated into this foreign country that you begin to regard it as your true home. Your allegiance wavers, and you gradually compromise your position as an ambassador, becoming increasingly ineffective in representing the best interests of your own country.

We must never become too much at home in this world or we will become ineffective in serving the cause of the kingdom we are here to represent. We are aliens, strangers, and pilgrims on earth. Peter wrote, *"Live out your time as foreigners here in reverent fear"* (1 Peter 1:17, NIV). Another Bible translation uses the words *"strangers and pilgrims"* (KJV).

Our daily choices determine what will happen in the future. What we do in this life and in our business is of eternal importance.

Pilgrims are unattached. They are travelers—not settlers—aware that the excessive accumulation of things can distract. Material things are valuable to pilgrims, but only as they facilitate their mission. Things can entrench us in the present world, acting as chains around our legs that keep us from moving in response to God. When our eyes are too focused on the visible, they will be drawn away from the invisible. *"So we fix our eyes not on what is seen, but on what is unseen, since what is seen is temporary, but what is unseen is eternal"* (2 Corinthians 4:18, NIV).

Pilgrims of faith look to the next world. They see their businesses and earthly possessions for what they are: useful for kingdom purposes, but far too flimsy to bear the weight of trust. Thomas à Kempis, author of *The Imitation of Christ,* said it this way: "Let temporal things serve your use, but the eternal be the object of your desire." Two principles concerning possessions help us gain a proper perspective of them.

Judgment

It's uncomfortable to think about judgment. But because our Lord loves us so deeply, He wants us to realize what will happen in the future. For this reason, God revealed to us that we all will be judged according to our deeds: *"He has fixed a day in which He will judge the world in righteousness"* (Acts 17:31). All of us should live each day with this awareness: *"They will have to give account to him who is ready to judge the living and the dead"* (1 Peter 4:5, NIV).

God will judge us with total knowledge: *"Nothing in all creation is hidden from God's sight. Everything is uncovered and laid bare before the eyes of him to whom we must give account"* (Hebrews 4:13, NIV). Because His knowledge is total, *"Everyone will have to give account on the day of judgment for every empty word they have spoken"* (Matthew 12:36, NIV). His judgment extends to what is hidden from people. *"God will bring every deed into judgment, including every hidden thing, whether it is good or evil"* (Ecclesiastes 12:14, NIV).

The Bible teaches that all those who do not know Christ will be judged and sent to an indescribably dreadful place. *"I saw a great white throne and him who was seated on it . . . . And I saw the dead, great and small, standing before the throne . . . . Each person was judged according to what they had done. . . . Anyone whose name was not found written in the book of life was thrown into the lake of fire"* (Revelation 20:11-15, NIV).

Judgment of Believers

After they die, those who know Christ will spend eternity with the Lord in heaven, an unimaginably wonderful place. But what we seldom consider is that the entry point to heaven is a judgment.

Scripture teaches that all believers in Christ will give an account of their lives to the Lord. *"We will all stand before the judgment seat of God. . . . So then each one of us will give an account of himself to God"* (Romans 14:10, 12). The result of this will be the gain or loss of eternal rewards. In 1 Corinthians 3:13-15 we read, *"Their work will be shown for what it is, because the* [Judgment] *Day will bring it to light. . . . If what has been built survives, the builder will receive a reward. If it is burned up, the builder will suffer loss* (NIV)." Our works are what we have done with our time, influence, talents, and resources.

God's Word doesn't treat this judgment as just a meaningless formality before we get on to the real business of heaven. Rather, Scripture presents it as a monumental event in which things of eternal significance are brought to light.

Motivation and Rewards

Why should I follow God's guidance on operating a business and handling money when it's so much fun to do whatever I please with them? After all, I'm a Christian. I know I'm going to heaven anyway. Why not have the best of both worlds—this one *and* the next? Though few of us would be honest enough to use such language, these questions reflect a common attitude.

The prospect of eternal rewards for our obedience is a neglected key to unlocking our motivation. Paul was motivated by the prospect of eternal rewards. He wrote, *"I have fought the good fight, I have finished the course, I have kept the faith; in the future there is laid up for me the crown of righteousness, which the Lord, the righteous Judge, will award to me on that day"* (2 Timothy 4:7-8). The Lord appeals not only to our compassion but also to our eternal self-interest. *"Love your enemies, and do good, and lend, expecting nothing in return; and your reward will be great"* (Luke 6:35).

Unequal Rewards in Heaven

Some think, *I'll be in heaven, and that's all that matters.*

But hold on—it's not that simple.

On the contrary, Paul spoke about the loss of reward as a *terrible loss,* and the receiving of rewards from Christ as a phenomenal gain. Not all Christians will have the same rewards in heaven.

John Wesley said, "I value all things only by the price they shall gain in eternity." God's kingdom was the reference point for him. He lived as he did, not because he didn't treasure things but because he treasured the right things. We often miss something in missionary martyr Jim Elliot's famous words, "He is no fool who gives what he cannot keep to gain what he cannot lose." We focus on Elliot's willingness to sacrifice, and so we should. At the same time, however, we often overlook his motivation for gain. What separated him from many Christians wasn't that he didn't want treasure, but that he wanted *real* treasure. Remember, God loves you deeply. Because He wants the best for you throughout eternity, God has revealed that today's generosity and service for Him will pay off forever.

Impacting Eternity Today

Our daily choices determine what will happen in the future. What we do in this life and in our business is of eternal importance. We only live on this earth once. *"It is appointed for men to die once and after this comes judgment"* (Hebrews 9:27).

There is no such thing as reincarnation.

You will not come back as this or that.

In fact, you won't come back at all. The Bible says that you will go forward to one of two destinations.

Once our life on earth is over, we will never have another chance to move the hand of God through prayer, to share Christ with a business associate who doesn't know the Savior, to give money to further God's kingdom, or to help the needy.

I loved playing Little League baseball as a young boy. We played on a huge field with towering fences in the outfield. Years later, shortly after my father died, I spent the day walking around my old hometown, reflecting on his life. When I visited the baseball field, I was shocked. It was so *small!* I could actually step over the outfield fences. While standing there, a thought struck me: Many of those things that seem so large and important to us today shrink to insignificance in just a few years.

When I am face to face with Christ and look back on my life, I want to see that the things in which I invested my time, creativity, influence, and money are big things to Him. I don't want to squander my life on things that won't matter throughout eternity.

What are the business choices facing you now? How does an eternal perspective influence your decisions? Martin Luther said his calendar consisted of only two days: "today" and "that Day." May we invest all that we are and have today in light of *that* day.

EIGHTEEN

You Can Know God

Iwas 28 years old when I started meeting with several young business-men. It wasn't long before I was impressed by their business savvy. But more than that, I was attracted by the quality of their lives. I didn't know what they had, but whatever it was, I wanted it.

These men spoke openly of their faith in God. I had grown up going to church, but the religion I had seen modeled during those years meant nothing to me as an adult. I had concluded it was only a fairy tale until a friend described how I could enter into a *personal* relationship with Jesus Christ. He explained several truths from the Bible I had never understood before.

God loves you and wants you to know Him.

God desires a close relationship with each of us. *"For God so loved the world, that He gave His only begotten Son, that whoever believes in Him shall not perish, but have eternal life"* (John 3:16). *"I [Jesus] came that they may have life, and have it abundantly"* (John 10:10).

Perhaps this example will help you understand His love. In the 1992

Olympics in Barcelona, Spain, Great Britain had a runner named Derek Redmond who had dreamed all his life of winning the gold medal in the 400-meter race. As the gun sounded for the semifinals, Derek knew he was running the race of his life. Then, tragically, as he entered the backstretch, Redmond felt pain shoot up the back of his right leg. A torn hamstring sent him sprawling face down on the track.

Instinctively, Derek struggled to his feet in excruciating pain and began hopping on one leg toward the finish line. Suddenly a large man came bounding from the stands. Flinging aside security guards, he made his way onto the field and threw his arms around Derek. It was Jim Redmond, Derek's father. "Son, you don't have to do this," he said.

"Yes, Dad, I do," Derek assured him.

"All right then, let's finish this together," said the older man. And that's exactly what they did. With the son's head frequently buried in the father's shoulder, they made it to the end of the race as the crowd rose to its feet, weeping and cheering![1]

Derek Redmond didn't win the gold medal in the Olympics. But he won something far more valuable. He walked away from the race with the memory of a father who was not only in the stands cheering but who loved him too much to watch him suffer from a distance—a father who came down out of the stands and entered the race with him, staying beside him every step of the way.

We have a heavenly Father who watches us with eyes of love and affection. He is our Abba Father-God who cared for us too deeply to stay in heaven, looking down on us, watching us fall and fail. Instead, He came down out of the stands and into our race in the person of His precious Son, Jesus Christ. And He is committed to staying in this race with us until we have safely crossed the finish line.[2]

Unfortunately, we are separated from God.

God is holy—which simply means God is perfect, and He can't have a relationship with anyone who is not perfect. My friend asked if I had ever sinned—done anything that would disqualify me from perfection. "Many times," I admitted. He explained that every person has sinned, and the consequence of sin is separation from God. *"All have sinned and fall short of the glory of God"* (Romans 3:23). *"Your sins have cut you off from God"* (Isaiah 59:2, TLB).

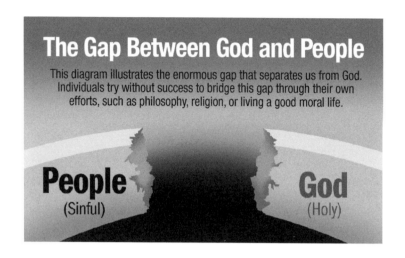

The Gap Between God and People

This diagram illustrates the enormous gap that separates us from God. Individuals try without success to bridge this gap through their own efforts, such as philosophy, religion, or living a good moral life.

People (Sinful)

God (Holy)

God's only provision to bridge this gap is Jesus Christ.

Jesus Christ died on the cross to pay the penalty for our sin, bridging the gap between God and us. Jesus said, *"I am the way, and the truth, and the life; no one comes to the Father but through Me"* (John 14:6). *"God demonstrates His own love toward us, in that while we were yet sinners, Christ died for us"* (Romans 5:8).

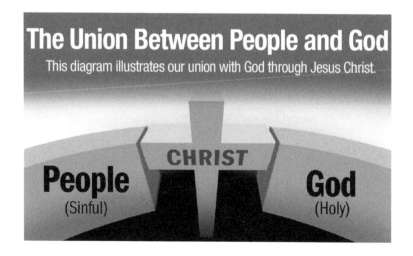

The Union Between People and God

This diagram illustrates our union with God through Jesus Christ.

CHRIST

People (Sinful)

God (Holy)

This relationship is a gift from God.

My friend explained that by faith I could receive the free gift of a relationship with God. *Free gift?* The transaction seemed unfair to me. I had learned in business that a transaction happens only when both sides are convinced they're getting more than they are giving up. But now I was being offered a relationship with God, and it was free! *"It is by grace you have been saved, through faith—and this is not from yourselves, it is the gift of God—not by works, so that no one can boast"* (Ephesians 2:8-9, NIV).

I had only to ask Jesus Christ to come into my life to be my Savior and Lord. So I did! As my friends will tell you, I'm a very practical person—if something doesn't work, I stop doing it. I can tell you from more than forty years' experience that a relationship with God is real. And it is available to you through Jesus Christ.

Nothing in life—and I mean this with everything in me—compares with knowing Christ personally. We can experience true peace, joy, and hope when we know Him. It's the only way you can enjoy a truly successful business career.

If you want to know God and aren't certain whether you have this relationship, I encourage you to receive Jesus Christ right now. Pray a prayer similar to the one I prayed: "God, I need You. I'm sorry for my sin. I invite Jesus to come into my life as my Savior and Lord, and to make me the person you want me to be. Thank You for forgiving my sins and giving me the gift of eternal life."

You might have an enormously successful business, but without a relationship with Christ, it won't have any lasting value. If you asked Christ into your life, you have made the most important decision anyone could ever make. I urge you to find a church that teaches the Bible, one where you can begin to learn what it means to follow Jesus Christ.

NINETEEN

Finishing Well

The signature line waited at the bottom of the contract. Scribbling the name his parents gave him 52 years earlier would give him enough cash to have the freedom to do whatever he wanted.

All he had to do was sign.

He could build the life of his dreams: more time with family, and options for each day that didn't start with a trip to the office at the crack of dawn.

All he had to do was sign.

"Tomorrow is the day," Rogers Kirven said to his two friends who had sold their companies a few years earlier. The trio met at a restaurant to celebrate the pending sale. It had been some time since they had seen each other, and Kirven walked in expecting pats on the back. Two hours later, he walked out terrified.

"The first thing they told me was that they had new wives," Kirven said. "I'd known one of them for fifteen years and another for seven. Both of them cashed out to spend more time with their families." The conversation bounced around from their new homes to their skiing and golf, never landing on anything meaningful.

As they walked out of the restaurant, Kirven asked his friend of fifteen years, also a follower of Christ, "Was this the best thing you ever did in your life?"

His friend shook his head in confusion and said, "I don't know. I don't think so."

These hard working individuals had lost their focus on what is important in life. Their relationship with Christ was too immature to tolerate this change. In short, their character was not sufficiently developed. Godly character is the key to finishing well.[3]

Finishing well is rare.

When people ask evangelist Billy Graham how they can pray for him, he invariably responds, "Pray that I finish my life well and don't dishonor the Lord." He recognizes how rare it is for people to remain faithful to the Lord and engaged in fulfilling their calling to the end.

According to the late Dr. Howard Hendricks, of the 2,930 individuals mentioned in the Bible, we only know significant details of 100. Of those 100, only about one-third finished well. Of the two-thirds that did not finish well, most failed in the second half of their lives. Finishing well for those who are successful in business is especially challenging because of the options money can buy. Many of these can distract us from serving Christ.

Of the 2,930 individuals mentioned in the Bible, we only know significant details of 100. Of those 100, only about one-third finished well. Of the two-thirds that did not finish well, most failed in the second half of their lives.

Someone once said, "In your journey with the Lord, it's not how you start that matters. It's how you finish. What are you doing to become the one in three who reaches the finish line still serving Christ? You will need spiritual discipline to have a strong finishing kick when you hit the tape at age 65, 75, 85, or whatever age God calls you home."

"You see, it's *endurance* that determines whether a person will finish strong. And endurance is the byproduct of godly character. The Christian life isn't a 100-yard dash; it's a marathon. Long races don't require speed; they require grit, determination, a steady, sustainable pace, and finishing power."

As Scripture says, *"Therefore, since we have so great a cloud of witnesses surrounding us, let us also lay aside every encumbrance and the sin which so easily entangles us, and let us run with endurance the race that is set before us, fixing our eyes on Jesus"* (Hebrews 12:1-2).

Finish strong despite past mistakes.

As you read these words, you may think it's already too late for you to finish well. Perhaps you've made some big bone-head mistakes. Many of those who finished well in the Bible were guilty of terrible decisions. Abraham lied. Moses committed murder. David was an adulterer and a murderer. Peter denied Christ three times.

Finishing well doesn't mean finishing with a perfect record.

But it does mean learning from our mistakes, getting back on course, and pursuing Christ with our whole heart. We are to work hard in building the kingdom of God as long as we are physically and mentally able, despite any previous mistakes we may have made. Paul, the murderous persecutor of the early church, said it this way: *"One thing I do: forgetting what lies behind and reaching forward to what lies ahead, I press on toward the goal for the prize of the upward call of God in Christ Jesus"* (Philippians 3:13-14).

Finish strong despite your age.

Aging is an inevitable part of life. Age imposes certain limitations, but we need to embrace God's perspective. As John Quincy Adams was nearing the end of his life, a friend asked how he was doing. "John Quincy Adams is well, quite well," replied the former sixth President of the United States. "But the house in which he lives at present is becoming quite dilapidated. It's tottering upon its foundations. Time has nearly destroyed it. Its roof is pretty well worn out. It is becoming almost uninhabitable, and I think John Quincy Adams will have to move out of it soon. But he himself is quite well, quite well."

The Apostle Paul said it this way, *"For we know that if the earthly tent which is our house is torn down, we have a building from God, a house not made with hands, eternal in the heavens. For indeed in this house we groan, longing to be clothed with our dwelling from heaven"* (2 Corinthians 5:1-2).

As we age, we are encouraged to concentrate on developing a closer relationship with the Lord. *"Therefore we do not lose heart, but though our outer man is decaying, yet our inner man is being renewed day by day"* (2 Corinthians 4:16).

George Fooshee has mentored me for more than three decades. George and his wife, Marjean, are in their eighties. They are more in love with Christ and with each other than ever before. They continue to invest themselves in the lives of others in their city and around the world. The psalmist wrote, *"The righteous will flourish like a palm tree . . . They will still bear fruit in old age, they will stay fresh and green"* (Psalm 92:12, 14, NIV).

Think of all those who have led enormously productive lives in old age. While in their eighties:

– Moses led the children of Israel out of captivity.

– Winston Churchill wrote his four-volume *A History of the English-Speaking Peoples.*

– Peter F. Drucker wrote 16 books after his 80th birthday and taught his last class on business management at age 92.

A small group of us recently met with an 80-year old who has influenced scores of men and women around the world for Christ. He told us of his sorrow because his wife of more than 50 years had just died. For several years, he had been giving her around-the-clock care. Then he shared how the Lord has recently used him to lead a young girl to Christ. As he spoke, we were arrested by the joy that radiated from his face.

When one of us asked, "What are your aspirations in this season of your life?" he answered without hesitation, "To take another mountain for God, just as Caleb did." Old age is temporary—the decisive lap in the grand race of life. To finish well we need to invest our life to its fullest in serving Christ during our time on earth.

Exit Strategy

Dave Palmer had a dream: to work with his son, Adam, in a business of their own and have Adam someday succeed him as CEO. Adam had graduated from college top of his class with a degree in computer sciences and began working for a global software company. Five years later, Dave began Palmer Software, and his son joined him on day one.

Dave and the management team quickly recognized Adams' leadership potential. For the first ten years they intentionally rotated him through every department in the company, from software development to sales and customer service. The next move was promoting him to VP of Operations and inviting him to a seat on the board of directors.

"I consider my life worth nothing to me; my only aim is to finish the race and complete the task the Lord Jesus has given me"
(Acts 20:24, NIV).

Adam played a significant role in the international expansion of the company and the development of the software for handheld devices. Even more importantly, he successfully navigated the company through a crisis.

Hard work and patience paid off. With the full support of the leadership team, Dave's vision came true when the board unanimously elected his son CEO of Palmer Software.

Sooner or later all of us must execute an exit strategy from our business. There are four options business owners can consider:

- Succession—choosing a family member to lead the business.
- Succession—selecting a trusted employee or outside manager to lead the business.
- Sale—deciding on an outright sale of the business.
- Merger—agreeing to merge with another business.

Let's examine each of these options:

Succession

A Family Member

The benefit of transferring the business to a family member is that the business stays in the family. The challenge of passing it along this way is that it stays in family!

In the Bible, the parents usually bequeathed businesses to their children. *"The LORD has greatly blessed my master* [Abraham], *so that he has become rich; and He has given him flocks and herds, and silver and gold, and servants and maids, and camels and donkeys. Now Sarah my master's wife bore a son to my master in her old age, and he has given him all that he has"* (Genesis 24:35-36).

> **There is only one reference to retirement in the Bible, and it applied to the Levites working in the tabernacle. There is no scriptural basis for retiring and adopting a life of leisure.**

Growing up around the business, the younger generation should understand its heritage and culture. Too often, however, the new leadership has not been mentored properly, and they don't really know the business or how to be an effective leader. Perhaps the new leader just doesn't have the capacity to lead well.

And then there are the challenges of a new family member leading the business while other members are either employees or passive owners. It's easy for family relationships to become frayed and damaged. If you choose a family member to succeed you, it is imperative for the new leader to have the written responsibility and the authority to lead. It is wise to seek counsel and help in the process from those experienced in succession. And as difficult as it is to address this, should the chosen family member need to be terminated from the job, make certain you have the process in writing.

Succession

A Trusted Employee or Outside Manager

If a qualified family member isn't available to assume leadership, and you decide not to sell or merge the business, it will be necessary to hire someone to manage it. This hiring decision will be one of the most important the family will ever make, so don't be hasty.

If you have been grooming someone on staff for this role, you should already know their values, work habits, and leadership capabilities. If no one on staff can assume this role, you will need to recruit someone from the outside.

Develop a clear job description that contains all your expectations. Enter into a written agreement with any one you choose, including the process of termination if they are unsuitable for the position. Once again, it's wise to seek advice from those experienced in this type of succession.

Sale

For a host of reasons, it may be smart to sell the business. In many ways, this is the easiest path to take once the sale is consummated. Often, the seller hopes that the new owner will maintain the values and culture of the business and that faithful employees will be retained. However, this is rarely the case.

Merger

In a merger, you bring two or more businesses together to become one. The biggest single issue to decide upon: Who has control? I mean, who *really* has control when it comes to making tough decisions?

It's also important to determine if, when, and for how much you can sell your interest in the merged company if you later decide to sell. One of the most important considerations of a merger is to evaluate the values and culture of both organizations to determine if they will be compatible with each other.

Startups and Entrepreneurs

RETIREMENT AND YOUR DREAM

Our culture promotes the goal of retirement to pursue a life filled with leisure. Is this a biblical goal? In the parable of the rich fool, Jesus strongly rebukes the notion of a life of leisure and ease: *"I* [the rich fool] *will say to my soul, 'Soul, You have many goods laid up for many years to come; take your ease, eat, drink and be merry.' But God said to him, 'You fool!'"* (Luke 12:19-20).

Numbers 8:24 is the only reference to retirement in the Bible, and it applied specifically to the Levites working in the tabernacle. While people are physically and mentally capable, *there is no scriptural basis for retiring and becoming unproductive*—the concept of putting an older but able person "out to pasture." Don't let age stop you from finishing the work God has called you to accomplish. He will provide you with the necessary strength and mental clarity.

The Bible does imply, however, that the type or intensity of labor may change as we grow older—shifting gears to a less demanding pace to become more of an "elder seated at the gate." During this season of life we can use the experience and wisdom gained over a lifetime. If we have sufficient income to meet our needs apart from our business and jobs, we may choose to leave work to invest more time in serving others.

Carefully read what Peter said toward the end of his life. *"I consider it right, as long as I am in this earthly dwelling, to stir you up by way of reminder, knowing that the laying aside of my earthly dwelling is imminent, as also our Lord Jesus Christ has made clear to me. And I will also be diligent that at any time after my departure you may be able to call these things to mind"* (2 Peter 1:13-15).

Do the words *"stir you up"* and *"diligent"* give even the slightest hint of retirement? On the contrary, they communicate an active life.

Greg dropped out of college after his freshman year and soon started a business. When he was in his mid-40s he enrolled in what became the Compass study while in the midst of selling his business to a Fortune 500 company. For 25 years, he had shouldered the responsibility and stress of building his company without really having sufficient capital. His objective was to sell out and live a more relaxed life with plenty of time for playing golf.

During the study, Greg discovered that the Lord discouraged retirement, so he began praying for the Lord to show him what he should do. I'll never forget the joyful expression on his face when he came to class and announced what he sensed God wanted him to do: Build businesses so that by the time he died the enterprises would be giving $1 million a *day* to the work of Christ!

I don't know if Greg will achieve this God-given dream. But I do know that he is engaged like never before in an exciting walk of faith with Christ. He is having a massive influence on his employees and is funding ministries around the world that serve needy women and children.

What is your God-given dream—your calling? Is it something that is beyond your capabilities? Well, guess what? God delights in stretching us out of our comfort zones by asking us to attempt something that is doomed to failure—unless He pulls it off. If you aren't certain of God's calling, I encourage you to pray. Ask Him to make it clear. May we all be able to echo what the Apostle Paul wrote in Acts 20:24, *"I consider my life worth nothing to me; my only aim is to finish the race and complete the task the Lord Jesus has given me"* (NIV).

Thank you for your investment of time reading *Business God's Way*. I pray that it will help you succeed in business. But far more than that, I hope you have grown even closer to Jesus Christ.

Business Plan

You will now focus on Crisis Preparation and Exit Strategies. It's never too early to begin addressing these important issues, because once you have clarity, it will influence daily business decisions. As with the rest of the Business Plan, periodically review these issues to make adjustments based on changes that inevitably occur.

Crisis Preparation

The leader or a key person is unable or unwilling to serve.

Who are the key people in the business?

_____

_____

_____

Who would replace them and how well-equipped are they to assume these roles? What needs to be done to prepare for this possibility?

_____

_____

_____

If the leader or another key person were unable to perform, what would be the financial impact and impact on relationships with customers, vendors, lenders, etc.? What needs to be done to prepare for this crisis?

_____

_____

_____

***Natural disaster, major fire, theft, national financial upheaval, hacked
systems, or other major crisis***

What disasters could cause the most damage to your business?

_____

_____

_____

What should you do to prepare for these disasters or crises?

_____

_____

_____

Exit Strategy

If you have decided upon an exit strategy (groom a successor, sell or
merge the business, etc.), describe it.

_____

_____

_____

If you have an exit strategy, what preparation have you made or do you
need to make to successfully implement it?

_____

_____

_____

If you do not have an exit strategy for the business or for you personally,
describe your plan to design one.

_____

_____

_____

Looking Back at Section 6: Finishing Well

React: Let's talk about it

1. Why do you think it is important to realize that God loves you and is in control of the situation when you face a crisis?

2. Share a crisis you have experienced and how God used it to help you grow closer to Christ.

3. Describe what you should do to prepare your business and personal finances for future challenges.

4. As you reflect on the brevity of life and the reality of eternity, answer this question thoughtfully: What three things do I want to accomplish most in my business and life during the rest of my time on earth?

5. What can you do in your business that would contribute most significantly to the cause of Christ?

6. Do you know your God-given dream for your business and life? If so, describe it.

Help — Online and other resources

Money, Possessions, and Eternity, by Randy Alcorn, Tyndale House Publishers, Wheaton, Illinois

Trusting God, by Jerry Bridges, 2008, NavPress, Colorado Spings, Colorado

Notes

Randy Alcorn contributed much of the "Eternity" portion of this Section from his outstanding book, *Money, Possessions, and Eternity* (Tyndale House Publishers, Inc.) To learn more, visit www.epm.org.

[1] *Finishing Strong,* Steve Farrar, 1995, Multnomah Book

[2] *Dear Abba,* Claire Cloninger, 1997, Word Publishing

[3] *The Dark Side of Halftime,* Nichole Johnson, The Life@Work Journal, Volume 2, Number 6, Page 36